Antony Gormley

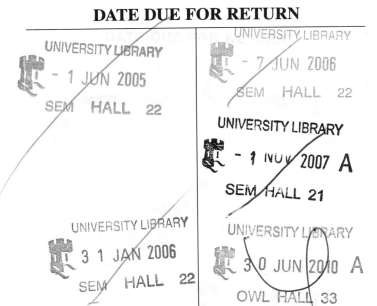

Seeds V 1987/93

Antony Gormley

Malmö Konsthall

Tate Gallery Liverpool

Irish Museum of Modern Art

Malmö Konsthall
18 September – 31 October 1993
Sponsored by Optiroc, Sweden

Tate Gallery Liverpool
20 November 1993 – 6 February 1994
Sponsored by:

IBSTOCK

with the support of The Henry Moore Foundation

Irish Museum of Modern Art
14 April – 19 June 1994

Contents

Still Falling 1991

Preface

It is with great pleasure and excitement that we mount this exhibition of Antony Gormley's work – the most comprehensive to date. In it we show the development of his pioneering work from the body; the terracotta field, the concrete pieces, the abstract iron expansion works, the new solid body forms and a few recent lead pieces. All but one of these works were made in the last four years and most are seen for the first time.

'Body' becomes a vibrant word when used to refer to Gormley's sculpture. What he proposes is that the human body is one amongst many (from the cellular to the celestial) and that all bodies are subject to the condition of sculpture: the relation of mass to space. In this return to the fundamentals of sculpture *through the body*, the work tests our received understanding of sculpture's European history.

It may be, on one level, that clay is the stuff that we are made of, and that sexuality, gender and race is what we are cast into. But what we are made *for* is the underlying question. The importance of Gormley's work is that it lives within this fundamental question.

This publication provides a timely overview of Gormley's achievement, documenting key developments since the mid 70s. We would like to thank Professor Stephen Bann for his wide-ranging essay positioning Gormley's revision of the human subject in sculpture within current philosophical and aesthetic debate.

This exhibition is the result of a three-way collaboration between Malmö Konsthall, Tate Gallery Liverpool and The Irish Museum of Modern Art in Dublin. The sculptures form different constellations in the three locations with principal works common to all. Whatever the differences and possibilities of each venue, this was a fantastic challenge to all those involved. Everyone has mobilized unsuspected resources of cooperation, curiosity and endurance but also shown their collective experience and skill in the demanding installations. We would all like to cordially thank Antony Gormley for inviting us along on this adventure.

Sune Nordgren   Lewis Biggs   Declan McGonagle
Malmö Konsthall   Tate Gallery Liverpool   Irish Museum of Modern Art

Acknowledgement

Antony Gormley would like to thank:

Niall O'Hare, Tom Yuill, Carl von Weiler, David Adams and Robert Turvey for assisting with the fabrication of the works. Arne Göransson, Ken Simons and the teams in all three venues for their help in installing the works.

The staff at Malmö Konsthall, students and teachers at Östra Grevie Folkhögskola and their indefatigable supervisor Oskar Ponnert for making 'European Field'. Optiroc, Sweden; Ingemar Åberj, Inge Haby and Lars Möller and their colleagues at the brick-works of Östra Grevie, Minnesberg and Bara.

The staff at Tate Gallery Liverpool, Adrian Plant, Derek Boak, Phyllis Richardson, John Rosier and all those at Sutton Community High School, St Helens who, with their energy and commitment, made 'Field for the British Isles' possible. Thanks to John Dunsford and John Carney of Ibstock Building Products Ltd. Also to Professor David Hamilton for help with the clay testing.

Special thanks to Michael Hinchcliff of Hargreaves Foundry and all his staff for their dedication, energy and expertise in making the expansion pieces. Also to Nigel Downs of H Downs and Co for his help in developing the solid iron body forms.

Herman Lelie, Judith Nesbitt and Jemima Pyne for their work on the catalogue and David Ward and Jan Uvelius for taking the photographs.

Salvatore and Caroline Ala for their consistent support over the last ten years and Claes Nordenhake for introducing his work to the public in Sweden.

Finally an expression of deep gratitude to his wife Vicken Parsons without whose constant collaboration the work would not be possible.

Learning to see: an introduction

Lewis Biggs

I celebrate myself, and sing myself,
And what I assume you shall assume,
For every atom belonging to me as good belongs to you.

Walt Whitman *Song of Myself*

A biographical approach to Antony Gormley's work would be justified, if for no other reason, by the fact that much of his sculpture is based on his own body[1]. Many of his sculptures are, literally, an embodiment of the artist. As a person, he has an immense capacity for enjoying life physically and intellectually: an ability to keep both his head in the clouds and his feet on the ground. His grandfather was a Catholic from Derry whose family had been dispossessed by the English. Like many Irish, he was staunchly pro-German during the 1914–18 war, but later married an English woman and settled in Walsall. His son, Antony's father, remained highly influenced by his Irish heritage and his strict Catholic upbringing all his life, and when he married a German physiotherapist from a Lutheran family she converted to Catholicism. Both Antony's parents were culti-vated and intellectually questioning people, more able to feel at home where they lived among the émigrés of Hampstead than among the English.

Antony was brought up a Catholic, attending a Benedictine boarding school, and the universalising impulse of Catholicism, along with its spiritual disciplines, have continued to shape his outlook. He was close to his German grandmother, a warm personality who was very 'nature centred' and conscious of healthy living. During his childhood in Hampstead, Antony often went to stay with his German grandparents in Worcestershire, and later in the Black Forest when they returned to Germany in the early 1960s. Their respect for the material world and its organic processes found expression in his belief in the body as the ground of experience, the temple of life. So while his Catholic upbringing and schooling nourished a certain idealistic and spiritual discipline, he also inherited an impulse to celebrate the direct experience of being in the world, and the primacy of sense

Sleeping Place 1974

experience as a form of knowledge. This intellectual inheritance, the bequest of two generations, formed by a commingling of Irish and German, of Catholicism and rationalism, constitutes a kind of open-ended creative space which Antony Gormley has sought to give form to, through his life and work.

The desire to transcend the limitations of his schooling was perhaps the major impetus he brought to his studies – first archaeology and anthropology, then art history – as an undergraduate at Trinity College, Cambridge. Besides everything that a university education in the late 1960s provided, Cambridge also gave Gormley his first exposure to the art world. Through friendship with Mark Lancaster (and then Michael Craig-Martin, both artists-in-residence at Kings' College) he met leading British and American artists, including Keith Milow, Richard Smith and Barry Flanagan. Many of his student friends were architects, and with others he became involved in film-making. During the next three years, spent in India, he took a close interest in Buddhism and studied Vipassana meditation with a Burmese teacher called Goenka, an experience which has had a lasting influence on him. It was at this point he decided to become a sculptor.

While at Cambridge he had showed his independence from current fashion by writing a thesis on the twentieth century mystic Stanley Spencer, whose painting was at that time largely ignored by the art market, academics and artists alike. In so doing, he signalled his desire to align himself with an ancient artistic tradition in which angels can still be angels, as much for Rilke as for Dante, as much for Spencer as for Piero della Francesca. Stanley Spencer, in Gormley's words, subscribed to 'the idea of life as *immersion*' and 'the

Open Door 1975

development of human consciousness as [life's] purpose'[2]. This is clearly also a statement of Gormley's own beliefs. If his aim, as an artist, is to contribute to the development of human consciousness, how is this to be achieved? His response is that art is 'an instrument for thinking', or perhaps (since thinking cannot be divorced from being) a catalyst for new states of being.

On his return from India, Gormley began a three year degree course in sculpture at the Central School of Art, London, but moved after one year to Goldsmith's College. At this time he made a group of works by draping cloth soaked in plaster over lying bodies, such as 'Sleeping Place', 1974. They were prompted by memories of people sleeping in stations in India wrapped entirely in cloth, but the sculptural interest in the resulting shape comes from the fact that it both exposes and hides the body within. These sculptures were already preoccupied with 'edges'[3], meditations on the way in which a single membrane may both insulate and connect, conceal and reveal.

'Open Door', 1975 was made by sawing a panel door vertically into thin strips which were then turned through ninety degrees and reassembled. It remains recognisably a door, but it is simultaneously both closed and open. It might also be seen as the 'Platonic idea' of a door along with its physical presence, or perhaps the secret 'innards' of a door along with its purpose – readings which suggest that the visible world cannot be taken at face value. In this way the work could be placed in dialectical relation to minimalism, then at the height of its influence, in which the 'primary structures' of André, Judd or LeWitt asserted that perception is everything, that what you see is all there is.

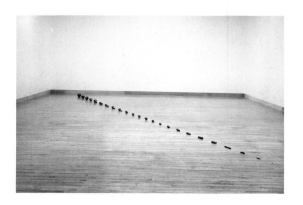

Fruits of the Earth 1978–9

Natural Selection 1981

Gormley's post-graduate studies were at the Slade School of Art. His sculptures from this period, several of which have survived, show him continuing to use everyday materials presented in such a way as to accept and play on whatever associations they commonly evoke. For instance, 'Last Tree', 1979 is a section of tree trunk carved away to reveal the lines of growth and, in the centre, the miniature 'original' of the tree, the sapling in its first year of growth. It undermines the proverb by giving us both the wood *and* the trees. It presents a slice through time: the past and the present along with a suggestion of the future of a tree. It presents an organic view of the world, a vision in which the microcosm, the seed, is present and equal with the macrocosm, the forest, and the individual related to the species.

On his arrival at the Slade, Gormley began to use lead as a sculptural material and it has remained of central importance to him ever since, both for practical reasons (it is both malleable and durable) and for its physical and associative qualities (its relationship with light, mass and its quality as an insulator and protector from radioactivity). 'Fruits of the Earth', 1978–9 consists of a bottle of Chianti, a revolver and a machete wrapped in layers of lead until each began to resemble an egg (seed or foetus). In this meeting of the artificial and the natural, the cultural artefacts' discrete identity has been neutralised by the lead casing; like a grain of sand in an oyster, the irritant is transformed. A more elaborate work on the same theme is 'Natural Selection', 1981, a line of alternating artificial and natural objects, ranging in size from a pea to a football, encased in lead. It proposes that the artificial and the natural are equally part of the evolutionary process.

Last Tree 1979

Bed 1980–1

Land, Sea and Air I 1977–9

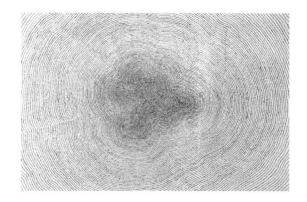

Exercise Between Blood and Earth 1979/81 (detail)

In April 1980 Gormley took part in his first international exhibition, *Nuove Immagine*, in Milan. He was represented by 'Land, Sea and Air I', 1977-9, 'Open Door', 1975 and the drawing 'Still Running', 1979, (re-made in 1981 in earth colours and re-titled 'Exercise Between Blood and Earth'), in a section of the exhibition called 'Archetypes'. The exhibition celebrated the plurality of approaches of the younger generation, but ecological and cross-cultural impulses were strongly represented. It had been arranged in the aftermath of the success of the Italian Transavanguardia, a number of young artists who shared a figurative approach in the late 1970s at a time when this was still unfashionable.

In June of the same year he married the painter Vicken Parsons, and they bought a dilapidated house in South London. It was their home and studios, and required a great deal of labour to make it weatherproof. Here Gormley made 'Bed', 1980-1, from waste 'Mother's Pride' white sliced bread which had been returned unsold to the factory. 'Bed' carries on it the duplicated imprint of the artist's own body, eaten out by him from a 'mattress' of bread (the slices were preserved by soaking them in wax). Although in some sense a marriage bed, it has often been remarked that it evokes a tomb in which the lying figures are seen in imprint rather than in effigy.

In the summer of 1981 Gormley exhibited four sculptures and a drawing on the upper floor of the Whitechapel Art Gallery in London. The chalk drawing was the life-size 'Exercise Between Blood and Earth', 1979/81, the image of a running man repeatedly inscribed like the ring marks in a tree trunk, or a finger print. 'Room', 1980, consisted of

Room 1980

Jacob Epstein *Elemental* 1932

Three Ways: Mould, Hole and Passage 1981

the artist's clothing shredded to ribbons and the ribbons tied to form an enclosure between four posts. Here also the body is implied, if not delineated, and related to a specific space. Common to all these early works is Gormley's approach to the body by its absence. And although his work appeared to change radically in the last months of 1981 and spring of 1982, this absence of the actual body – within a work which is a sign for the human person – has remained a central strategy for him until the present.

The change in Gormley's work coincided with his participation in a landmark exhibition of *British Sculpture in the 20th Century* held at the Whitechapel Art Gallery in Autumn 1981, the first such survey to be attempted for many years. It included an alabaster sculpture by Jacob Epstein called 'Elemental', 1932, a figure crouched in a foetal position, looking up. Gormley was deeply impressed with this sculpture – perhaps affected by the fact that his first child was to be born in April 1982 – and it became one of the catalysts for him to concentrate more fully on the body as his main subject[4].

'Mould', 1981 (which forms part of 'Three Ways: Mould, Hole and Passage'), was Antony Gormley's first lead body sculpture, the prototype of a working method forming a large part of his output: '...*the sculptures are made from my own body. Each work starts with a real body in real time and comes from a real event. It is not dissimilar to a photograph. I adopt the position which I have selected for a sculpture and am wrapped in scrim, which is an open-weave jute cloth, and plaster. Because the plaster dries quickly, within ten minutes, the work is divided into different sections... The whole process takes about an hour, perhaps an hour and a half. Then I am cut out of my mould and it is reassembled... It is a bit like going to the hospital to have an X-ray. Breathe in and hold it, the technician says. You are aware that there is a transition, that something that is happening within you is gradually registering externally. But for accuracy, it must be a moment of stillness, of concentration. I am trying to make sculpture from the inside, by using my body as the instrument and the material. I concentrate very hard on maintaining my position and the form comes from this concentration*[5].

Once he has reassembled the mould and worked on the form, he strengthens it with a thin layer of fibreglass. Then roofing lead is beaten into place over the contours of the mould until a complete skin is achieved, and the lead plates soldered or welded together. This complete skin therefore hovers something between one quarter of an inch to several inches above the place where the artist's actual skin once was. The sculpture is literally a case for a person, analogous to the sloughed skin of a snake or discarded chrysalis.

In the majority of the body cases the sheets of lead (on one occasion copper, and more recently cast iron) have been soldered, or welded, with the seams running true to the absolutes of horizontal and vertical, rather than along any internal axis of the figure. Thus the anatomical structure of the body is replaced by a structure of the surface: subjective states are carried by objective mapping.

The idea of self-knowledge through an interior relationship with the body in action is familiar to athletes, actors or musicians. For instance, Yehudi Menuhin practised yoga, 'to induce', as he said, 'a primary sense of measure and proportion. Reduced to our own body, our first instrument, we learn to play it, drawing from it maximum resonance and harmony ... we refine and animate every cell as we return daily to the attack, unlocking and liberating capacities otherwise condemned to frustration ... our fundamental attitudes to life have their physical counterparts in the body'[6].

'Land, Sea and Air II', 1982 another three-figure work, evokes the relationship we establish with our surroundings through our senses. One is crouching with ear to the ground, one standing upright and gazing to the far level horizon, and the third kneeling with head raised, as if breathing deeply. Although the senses are located in the skin, on the periphery of the 'person', as it were, we know that they are active at a distance from the body as much as internally to it. The free passage of information across the barrier of the skin is an indication of the fact that our being is similarly unfettered by our visible boundary. We can aspire to be both here and there simultaneously. These sculptures are

Land, Sea and Air II 1982

about being in a space, about the whole sense field. The work becomes a way of sensing space.

The single figure has continued to be central to Gormley's sculpture. One recent work is 'Learning to See', 1991. Standing in front of it we feel drawn to take account of ourselves. On one level this is no different from the feeling of meeting a new person. But this is not a person, it is the artist's presence removed from the flow of time. The 'measuring up' and 'affirmation' are made in relation, rather, to some felt potential of us as viewers. It is initially a physical process. We notice the horizontal and vertical seams which relate so strongly to architecture or landscape. We become conscious of the way we are standing, whether upright or leaning, one leg forward or both together, and so on. The lack of surface features, and the concentration of the pose, quickly produce an empathic response drawn from the reservoir of our own feelings. As Yehuda Safran suggests: '... these sculptures do not distract us with likeness, they have no distinctive feature, they make us aware of the whole. They invite our particularity, our souls are invited to dwell in these bodies...'[7].

When Rilke remarked, in his essay on Rodin, 'Whoever had the power of seeing and producing all forms, would he not ... give us all spiritual emotions?'[8], he was articulating a belief in the co-extension of the material and spiritual. Whereas it was possible, up to the beginning of this century, to maintain that the human being and the human image had 'integrity' (and mirrored the essential integrity of the cosmos) our minds – if not our bodies – tell us now that personal and epistemological integrity are at best under threat, at worst illusory. A note in Gormley's sketchbook of 1984 seems to reaffirm Rilke's contention: '*My body contains all possibilities. What I am working towards is a total identification of all existence with my point of contact with the material world: my body ... Part of my work is to give back immanence both to the body and to art*'.

Towards the end of the decade, Gormley developed further new ways of working. Alongside the continued development of the lead figures and their counterparts in iron, there were works in clay, concrete, iron 'expansion pieces' and lead boxes. Each adopts a different strategy but reflects on the same range of concerns: how to present simultaneously both the earthly condition of the body and its imaginative or spiritual transcendence.

Vehicle 1987

Peer 1984

'Vehicle', 1987, can be seen as a surrogate human being in much the same way as medieval cathedrals were built in the image of man. (The modern solo glider is so precisely designed as an extension of the human body that it needs the body's weight to enable it to fly). Its title, 'Vehicle', draws attention to what is being transported as well as how. This is not the *idea* but the *embodiment* of flight. It shows the human soul in its aspiration.

A group of works of the late 1980s is a quartet of pairs of 'boxes'. Each pair appears to link one of the organs of sense (the sense of feeling is not represented) with an internal organ. 'The senses are a kind of reason', said St. Thomas Aquinas (as paraphrased by Eric Gill), meaning that they lead us to reality[9]. 'Instrument' and 'Exposure', 1988/93 are a box with alabaster testicular or ovary-shapes on top and a box with eye holes. The sense of sight is apparently allied with the organs of reproduction. Together they might be thought to repeat the idea of 'Peer', 1983–4, making the connection between the two ends of the nervous system, the head looking at the tail.

A second pair is 'Body and Light', a brain cast in tree-resin resting on a box and

Instrument 1988/93 and *Exposure* 1988/93

'Meaning', a box with a mouth-hole, 1988/93 (p 75). These might be representations of the sense of taste and the organ of consciousness. In the third pair, 'Augur', two kidneys in brown alabaster resting on a box and 'Oracle', 1989/93 (p 76), a box with holes at the ears, hearing seems to be allied to the organ of purification. And in 'Bridge', a box with nostril-holes, and 'Centre', 1993 with a tree-resin heart placed on top (p 77), the sense of smell is juxtaposed with the organ of motivation or desire. These highly pungent works reduce the body to its essentials but the result of reduction is an abstracted notion of its 'spiritual' functions. Traditionally, Western medicine made connections between the internal organs (liver, pancreas etc) and the temperamental life through the 'humours'. But Gormley's lead boxes perhaps refer more easily to the yogic 'chakras', or centres of energy. In yogic thought, the three main paths of energy in the body run along the spinal column, and along two channels starting in the two nostrils and ending at the base of the spinal column. The chakras are distributed along the spinal chord where these three paths intersect, and are associated with (but not located in) specific organs. Four of the more important chakras are associated with the generative organs, the kidneys, the heart and the cranium.

Room for the Great Australian Desert 1989

Room II 1987

Taken together, this quartet of boxes reiterates the assertion that the way we make sense of the world relies on interior as much as exterior data. One commentator has noted that for Gormley, 'space... is not only external but includes the inner space given in thought, or in the lungs and other human organs which are connected with the outside by bodily orifices'[10]. Gormley relates a recurrent childhood reverie before sleep in which 'a match-box theatre space behind the eyes became an infinite wide extension of space in front of me'[11]. He has remained fascinated by the way that consciousness can be so much larger than the space which contains it, by the relation between the infinite extension of the imagination and the physical constraint of our senses. We can be both at home in the body and mental travellers at the same time.

The concrete works are concerned with concentrated space. 'Room II', was made to show at the Serpentine Gallery in February 1987, and consists of vertically stacked cubes of concrete (with two inch thick walls) and holes left for the mouth, ears, anus and penis. It is, as the title suggests, a piece of architecture: a cell for a human body. It reminds one of the Buddhist shrines into which a person may be bricked up, leaving only one point of communication with the outside, a hole through which food enters and excreta exits. In such an incarceration, sight would be hugely reduced in importance, while hearing would become acute. In the work of the same title, 1980 (p 18) the artist's clothes were shredded to create a fenced area or 'corral'. While the earlier work expanded the 'skin' of the person to the size of a room, in this piece the world is contracted to become the second skin of the person.

'Room for the Great Australian Desert', 1989, made during a residency in Sydney, was closely modelled on 'Room II'. It was conceived as a counterpart to 'Field for the Art

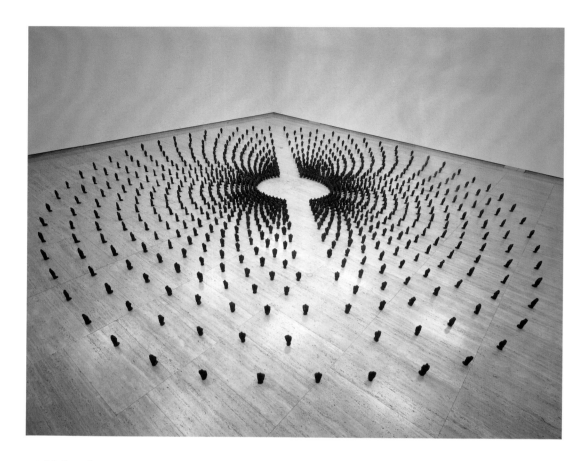

Field for the Art Gallery of New South Wales 1989

Gallery of New South Wales' 1989 – taking a concrete architectural 'place' to the vast red clay of the desert in the way that 'Field' brought the 'organic' clay into the formal architecture of the Gallery.

The later concrete works (pp 78–83), forgo the alliance of architectural space with body space and are closer to the lead moulds: they are blocks, containing the space vacated by the artist's person. 'Flesh', 1990, 'Immersion', 1991, 'Sense', 1991 and 'Home of the Heart III', 1992 are concentrated catalysts for sensing space. Using mass to describe the spatial relationship between the artist's body and the condensed interior of the early concrete rooms, these blocks set up a powerful dynamic with the space in which they are shown, engaging the body of the viewer in the interface between the space in the room and the space inside the block; the walls of the room and the rough surfaces of the block.

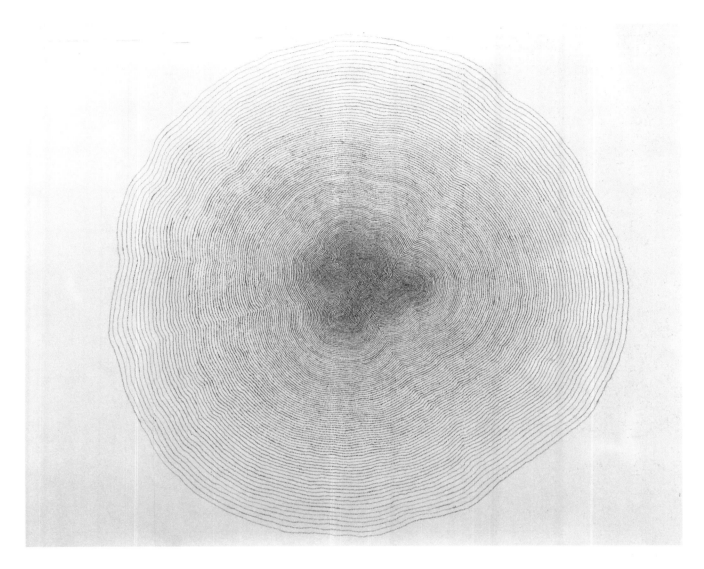

Exercise Between Blood and Earth 1979/81

In 1990 Gormley began a group of cast iron 'expansion' works (pp 84–91), which decisively break the human scale of much of his sculpture. 'Still Running', 1990/3, is a reprise of the drawing of the same title of 1979 (above, retitled). A mould was made of the artist in a running position, and then a second mould was made by measuring out a fixed distance from all points of the skin, an exact enlargement which (like the drawing) nevertheless generalises the shape of the artist beyond appearance. The expansion works represent a significant development in Gormley's work for their attempt to replace the body in the natural hierarchy of forms *without* recourse to the identification of the body. In a mysterious conversion, it is as if the aureole of the body is made solid and impenetrable.

Body 1991/3 (plaster)

Gormley has shown a preference for his body works to be photographed out of doors – in rural landscape, but also in urban or industrial settings. He has also made sculptures specifically for exterior and non-gallery sites. The development of 'Field' from the Australian version owes as much to 'monumental' as to gallery sculpture. During 1988 Gormley invested considerable energy on a project for a 120 feet high building in the form of a standing man, to be built in brick for a site at a railway junction near Leeds known as the Holbeck Triangle. The project was never realised, but its central idea – the equivalence of clay bricks in the figure to cells in the body and so to individuals becoming the 'body' of the community – re-emerged in 'Field for the Art Gallery of New South Wales' (p 28). In this latter work, small clay figures are organised into a magnetic 'force field'[12], implying a greater whole within which the parts have their place, in the way that the individual has a place in a community. A further development of 'Field' was

The Brick Man (Model) 1987

Field 1991 (installation at Salvatore Ala Gallery, New York)

more specific in placing the artist himself within a particular community – made up of over sixty members of an extended family of brickmakers in Mexico. It has subsequently been made again in the Amazonian rain forest, in Malmö ('European Field', pp 100–3) and in St. Helens, near Liverpool ('Field for the British Isles'). The idea is simple: a group of people join together to turn clay into a myriad of small figures, which are then fired and stood up, like a crowd all facing the same way, to entirely fill a room. Each person is invited to form the work in their hands, one at a time, but because each person's hands are different, as is their use of them, the final figures are also unique. By working together the participants begin to sense themselves as a collective body, even if previously unknown to each other, and at the same time create an image of that collective body. The simplicity and elegance of the idea are matched by its visual and emotional impact. Minimalist sculpture emphasised material presence through seriality and scale (very often filling all the available space). In 'Field', each figure derives its scale and shape from the hand of the person making it, and its position in the final installation is likewise the result of intuitive process rather than a predetermined order. While using some of the strategies of minimalism to capture the senses, it subverts the impersonality of minimalism through emphasising the hand-built and unique nature of each unit.

The questions it evokes are both physical (the effect of population growth on our diminishing common resource, the earth) and metaphysical (the relation of the individual to the whole). But its most powerful suggestion, and one which is central to Gormley's work, is that we are witnessing something in the act of becoming. Waves of figures stretch out with the fullness of an ocean. Because they are small, like seedlings planted out, the figures suggest potential growth, a sense of becoming.

Notes

1. 'The development of the work is above all tied to my development as an individual'. Antony Gormley, in conversation with the author 15 March 1993.

2. 'Cookham's Present', in *Stanley Spencer: A Sort of Heaven*, Tate Gallery Liverpool, 1992, p 7.

3. In his exploration of myth *The Time Falling Bodies Take to Light* (a book Gormley found inspirational), William Irwin Thomson writes: 'Edges are important because they define a limitation in order to deliver us from it. When we come to an edge we come to a frontier that tells us we are now about to become more than we have been before', St Martins Press, New York, 1981, p 8.

4. Sandy Nairne, 'Such Stuff as Dreams are Made on', in *Antony Gormley*, Städtische Galerie Regensburg / Frankfurter Kunstverein, 1985, p 48.

5. Interview with Roger Bevan in *Learning to See*, Galerie Thaddaeus Ropac, Paris/Salzburg, 1993, p 34.

6. Yehudi Menuhin, introduction to B K S Iyengar, *Light on Yoga*, London, 1966, p 13.

7. Yehuda Safran, introduction to *Learning to See*, ibid., p 27.

8. Rainer Maria Rilke, 'Rodin', *Selected Works*, London, 1954, vol 1, p 140.

9. Eric Gill, *Art*, London, 1934, p 125. This sentence is underlined in Gormley's copy.

10. Veit Loers, 'Calling upon Matter', in *Antony Gormley*, Städtische Galerie Regensburg / Frankfurter Kunstverein, 1985, p 40.

11. In conversation with the author, 15 March 1993.

12. The viewer is invited to enter the work by the pathway and at the centre becomes the focus of the gazes of the 1100 pairs of eyes, similar to the relation of the sapling to the amphitheatre in 'Last Tree'.

Antony Gormley
Interview with Declan McGonagle

Declan McGonagle: *Why would you say you are a sculptor rather than any other kind of artist?*

Antony Gormley: When I started as a child it was as if learning to draw was the most important challenge that art had to offer. By the time I was fifteen or sixteen I had learnt a kind of drawing and from then on the challenge was in being able to make the illusions of the two-dimensional surfaces more and more convincing – in the end that wasn't enough. Once you accept that painting is an object in the world and that its relationship with the viewer is more important than being a window onto another world, you are already making sculpture.

Was it a conscious decision to be a sculptor?

In India, I realised that sculpture was, for me, a more profound way of challenging reality. But painting is still in some respects at the back of the work. Some of the recent work like 'Host' or 'Field' (pp 39, 53) treats the space of the room not dissimilarly to the space of the canvas; the frame of the room is not dissimilar to the frame of the canvas.

'Field' actually requires a threshold.

The use of the threshold is a kind of framing. But I hope what I've done with those works is test the implicitness of modernist field-painting. To actually go in the other direction: 'Field' makes life its subject. It re-opens the old window onto *our* world but from the side of the art. A gaze or an energy comes towards us and it is not polite.

The group of works you showed in an old prison building in Charleston's Spoleto Festival in 1991 seemed a very complete statement of your values and the forms you are now using.

For me Charleston was the first exhibition that dealt with the wider terms of the work. It was me looking back over the last ten years and taking the opportunity of that Old Jail building to set up contrasting energies of freedom and containment. Removing windows and all the electricity was very important so that, rather like we have done in the room in

Cord 1991 (Old City Jail, Charleston)

Dublin, time is engaged through the passage of natural light. Time passing in relation to the stillness of the objects in the room becomes an active principle into which the life of the viewer also becomes immersed. In Charleston it was lovely because the orientation of the building was axial and you had the passage of the sun from the West side to the East side that had different effects at different times – depending on whether it was illuminating the rich red of the terracotta pieces or, in the evening, shining through the windows over the room full of mud. There was an acoustic effect too. By losing its glazing, the building became a kind of ear through which the feeling of the interior became amplified by the outside being more present. You could hear birds singing and the children in the playground in the housing project that surrounded the prison. There was also a breath – the movement of the wind through the building giving it another kind of life. It was a liberation of a building about which the black people around it say, 'That's the place they used to lynch us'. I wanted to take the building and identify it as a body. I do feel that the way that we dwell in the body is like the way a body dwells in a building, which may be even more true of a prison. I then wanted to insert different objects and fields within it, changing from fluid to cellular, from condensed to expanded – the idea of passage was very important.

Learning to Think 1991 (Old City Jail, Charleston)

Three Bodies 1991 (Old City Jail, Charleston)

It's very unusual to have had the opportunity to show such a range of works which took the body from its primal slime through to another state.

I'm very glad you've picked up on that. The idea is that through the building I set up parameters of sensation and invitations to contemplation. So there was a contrast between the two levels: on the ground floor, mud that had passed through the fire and had been touched, and on the second floor, elevated primal ouse, pluff mud taken from Charleston harbour, mixed in sea water. The flooded room was another way of describing a Modernist Tabula Rasa, but with the idea that the potential for life was there. Sea water, organic mud, the smell of it, the sympathy that it had with the light – which again held a strong relationship to the lead pieces that were in the room opposite. Then on the other diagonal were these platonic bodies, three hollow steel balls four feet in diameter, which because they had been made from spun steel, had a vortex inscribed on their surface. So touching the surface of the earth you have the idea of a celestial body that has been brought into our realm, and then opposite and above were the five body cases passing through the ceiling – or hanging down from it. Here are corporeal bodies escaping from the normal conditions of a body: they could be rising, hanging, or perhaps floating

Host 1991 (Old City Jail, Charleston)

Fruit 1991 (Old City Jail, Charleston)

and seen from below like swimmers in a pool. As with all the insertions into architecture, the idea was to undermine the expected conditions of being-in-a-room: they are in the room but *not* in it at the same time.

The hexagonal back of the prison consisted of two iron-clad spaces. On one side I installed two expanded body cases linked across an existing plaster and brick partition by steel pipes that connected the genitals and mouths. It was like a huge fungal brain and had to be constructed in the cells. On the other side was a single bent copper pipe, open at one end, that passed through the ceiling – a kind of umbilicus connecting us to somewhere else.

You have used lead, concrete, iron and in 'Host' in Charleston, river mud, to make sculpture. Where does material and its manipulation sit in your preoccupations as an artist?

At a certain stage I accepted the Buddhist position; I wanted to deny desire. I saw desire in some way as a false economy of art. The desire to aesthetically possess or be possessed. Hence for the last ten years the preoccupation with enclosing things in an aesthetically neutral material. I chose lead for the same reason as Maillol did for his nudes; he wanted to have a tension between the sensuality of the form and the distancing effect of the material. In about 1984 I realised that clay was an important material. There was a time just after I moved into the new studio when it was just full of clay and I was trying to find a way of making that wasn't imposing an image on the material but allowing a one-to-one relationship between my body and the body of the clay. The forms arose naturally from the space between my hands; clay was another way of dealing with the flesh. Out of this the very first ideas of the 'Field' work came. I must have made several hundred before they had eyes and I then realised that eyes were life! Somehow that was a return to desire. With 'Field', joy in material contact is there: it is about touch and touch expressed for its own sake. Touch not just of my hands but of many people's hands. Gone was the feeling that in order to be serious there had to be extreme distance between the personal engendering of the work and its public showing.

It seems you did not allow yourself to enjoy the material, to be seduced or to exhibit that seduction in the final work, until recently. Did you find yourself getting to a point with material and then deliberately distancing yourself?

In the early 1980s I wanted my body to be the prime material. I didn't want the viewer to be seduced by the work for the wrong reasons, I wanted it to be a kind of objective appraisal of my relationship to the world. I am very aware that all dialectical thinking has limited use. We are setting up oppositions between unconditioned and conditioned attitudes but taking on the body was a desire to touch things deeper than at a dialectic level, which was different from a lot of my generation's attitudes to material and how material and meaning coalesce.

That sounds as if the distancing is possibly more than just material.

I can well remember, at five or six, the first feeling of not belonging, and wondering whether I was really the son of my mother or father or whether I was some kind of implant. I think I had this sense from very early on (that I got from my father because he was always coming back from India, Malaya or Australia or somewhere) of there being another place where things were different, and that was the place for me.

From the moment I escaped from monastic education I was looking for another world view. I left the sacraments, and yet up to that point, Catholicism had been the central moral and life-supporting structure and remains a vital witness, because it is something that needs replacing. I need to build something as strong as that.

Having had a religious, Catholic upbringing I recognise that impulse. Is your practice then built on the expression of anxiety rather than its resolution?

What you recognise in the pieces in Derry and I recognise in the 'Field' is a witnessing of our life but is in some sense also a judgement of it. A lot of the anxiety that I feel comes

Close III 1993

from the tensions between the chaos of daily life and the sense of judgement in the Catholic moral values with which I was indoctrinated at an early age. I was told as a child that I had the devil in me. Anxiety comes from feeling judged, from not being accepted. I want to start with things that just are, that cannot be judged because judgement does not alter them.

Do the works themselves enter the world as witnesses to this process, like 'Close' as an idea but also in its siting?

What I hope 'Close' does is test the notion of site as a fixed place with the idea that nothing is fixed.

As if material has coalesced momentarily in this form but is capable of melting again? The force being described in the piece is what allows us all to 'hold on' momentarily.

At this latitude we are spinning at 1000 kilometres per hour through space. Through the figure you feel the tension between the force of centrifuge (that threatens to fling us out into deep space) and the forces of gravity; that sympathy between bodies that keeps us stuck down. What 'Close' is, is a body holding on for dear life. What it describes is a fixed point in a shifting world.

The Royal Hospital
Kilmainham

There is an axis described within The Irish Museum of Modern Art, centred on a formal courtyard, which would provide an amazing context for 'Close'.

That's a great idea, kind of underplaying the idea of frame and yet at the same time acknowledging it.

The Royal Hospital building [which houses the Museum] and its formal gardens were constructed on ideas about ordering that shifting world. We establish order here and we defend it so we build formal gardens and we look out over the demesne. From the Great House we see the formal gardens but we must also see the wilderness beyond, in order to feel that we are 'holding on'. Order is emphasised by setting it against the wilderness.

Trying to hold on at a time of chaos, desperately trying to make something solid which is, in fact, moving.

This seems to be a period when things are moving very fast. Brian Friel once quoted Tyrone Guthrie talking about how he had spent an afternoon keeping the bush out of the yard and went on to say that, after all, that is what we are all doing, isn't it, keeping the bush out of the yard!

I think that for me the challenge of our times is to recognise that culture is an extension of nature: that art is a part of a natural system which leads us back to our nature in nature. All we have been saying up to now is a house needs a bog in order to feel its houseness, but in this formula the bog is always seen as the other, and what we have to recognise is the bog in us. I recently contributed a version of 'Close' to a Biennale in Japan where it is an alien presence in a dinosaur park of international style sculpture. I would say that it engages with the exposed nature of that site and therefore 'works'. The intimacy of the work is a point of experience in that place of bogginess, and high wind. My work has been characterised as trying to carry on traditions of the transcendent or the utopian, but I'm not sure about that. I think what it tries to do is talk about some base in a very confusing world by confronting the earth. Because 'Close' makes a relationship between itself and the earth, I think by implication the things that are on top of the earth in its vicinity are also implicated, and that includes the viewer.

So transcendental or utopian readings of your work are too easy?

Yes I think it is an easy reading because it suggests that through the work there is an image of release and I think it's more like ... the opposite.

Is it a doorway towards anxiety?

I don't think it is that, either. I'm not sure that it is a doorway. There are two lines of Bob Dylan's that might help: 'Death is not the end' and '90 miles an hour down a dead end street'. There is a kind of collective madness that is taking us towards a terminal point, but there is also a feeling that this bodily existence of ours is only one level of existence. But I don't know what the next thing is, and the work doesn't pretend to know what the next thing is, either. All I'm trying to do is materialise the uncertainty and to isolate some point of contact between consciousness and matter.

My eight year old son is starting to ask from the back of the car – if we are going to die what is the point of living?

What was your answer to that?

Tell me who has the answer to that?

Well the answer is being here.

So all you can do is be here? Our human condition is about unknowing and uncertainty rather than knowing?

Yes. I believe that whatever there is beyond is connected with what is here, and you can have a sense of dispersion of self when you sit for a while doing nothing but just being conscious of the body and feeling that attachment to body and self, me and mine disintegrate and you are able to experience energy rather than objects: that is freedom. Maybe people would call that death.

Have you described 'Field' in the last few sentences?

That's a very nice idea. The idea of *being a place* is rather like one consciousness being subsumed within a wider consciousness.

Would you make a distinction, then, between your use of the body and other current preoccupations with the body in the work of an artist like Kiki Smith, for instance, whom you feel sees the body as text?

Yes, I think her interest in the body is, in a way, analytical, but I think what's great about the way that she uses that analysis is that she recognises that the alimentary or neurological systems have a strong metaphoric meaning in terms of human society generally. But I still find the work plays on a peculiarly American phobia about the breakdown of the body or fear of disease – playing almost a doctoring role to that culture. I am not so concerned with recognition of the functions of the body. I am much more interested in the space that the body is. What is that space that you inhabit when you close your eyes?

It's interesting – this idea of work doctoring to a particular culture. Does your work doctor to any particular culture?

'Doctor Heal Thyself', is more my line, and that means finding the other half of life that my upbringing excluded me from – which is an encounter with the earth, the body and the unconscious. I believe in guardian angels. Your fate is not simply your own doing. You know my parents gave me the initials AMDG (Ad Maiorem Dei Gloriam): For the Greater Glory of God. I can remember, when I was about six, my father taking me to one of the factories in his charge, when he had a foundation stone laid with AMDG on it, and a cross, and the date, and saying 'This is yours'.

It must have looked like a tombstone.

A Case for an Angel III 1990

It did look like a tombstone. But the sense that the shape of my life was known some-where else was something that I grew up with, and is both a limitation and a kind of enabler, because I don't think I would have set off at eighteen into the unknown without a guardian angel.

So 'A Case for an Angel' is a declaration of faith?

'A Case for an Angel' is a declaration of inspiration and imagination. It is an image of a being that might be more at home in the air, brought down to the earth. On the other hand it is also an image of somebody who is fatally handicapped, who cannot pass through any door and is desperately burdened. When installed it is a barrier across the space, blocking out the light and blocking the passage of the viewer. The top of the wings are actually at eye level and describe a kind of horizon beyond which you can't see very much, and so you feel trapped and there is a sense of an invitation to assert yourself in the space against it. It is an attempt to re-invent an idea of the object against which you can pit yourself, as in a Serra or a Judd, but differently.

Are you trying to draw upon a tradition or continuum which predates the Renaissance, which is pre-modern and still viable?

Do you mean magic – how is that different from Modernism?

Well, the large scale exhibition at the Museum of Modern Art in 1984, 'Primitivism' and

Twentieth Century Art, *far from re-affirming the principles of Modernism, demonstrated its redundancy! To disconnect art from its social meaning, and value it only in terms of its formal properties, does a disservice to both the so-called 'primitive' practice and Modernist practice. Modernism (the idea that events result from human action) and magic (the pre-modern) may come in and out of focus in human history, but possibilities for both exist now. It's what makes this period particularly interesting, as we come to an end of particular values which ran from the Renaissance through the Reformation, the Enlightenment and nineteenth century Capitalism.*

There *is* a recuperation of both modernism and magic. This goes back to finding the other within. It's interesting in relation to the question: 'Is the work transcendent?'. 'A Case for an Angel' is not ironic. I do believe that we can be transported or be the agent of our own transcendence. Maybe transcendence is the wrong word – but the idea that flight, in gliding, depends on weight and its correct position, is fantastic. I like the marriage of anatomy and technology. It isn't a kind of Icarus – you know, little bird feathers. I want something that is very concrete. In terms of the idiom, you can see the technology and we know that it works. The expansion pieces are the opposite. They go the other way, and try to talk about the human extension into the organic world of cells and vegetables.

You have said that the body is a collection of systems, that these systems can connect with other elemental systems.

There are two ways of connecting with the elemental and one is technological and the other biological, and I think they are both valid, and both necessary. They both have to be made conscious – not extraction-orientated, integrational rather than exploitative and divisive.

You seem to make that very visible in 'Sovereign State' (pp 92–3) – the innards occupy more space than the material bodies you have created.

I wanted to make an image of power deposed. Of a king pushed to the floor, lying next to his support mechanism – which echoes his biological internal mechanism.

In expanding the body case, it began to look like an astronaut's suit. In destroying the hierarchy between the stratosphere and the earth, between the king and his subjects, one of the principle transitions of the work is to make the viewer himself the subject of the work, and that is also part of the sovereignty that the work depicts. Then I began to think more about the orifices and the necessary connections and I wanted to connect the

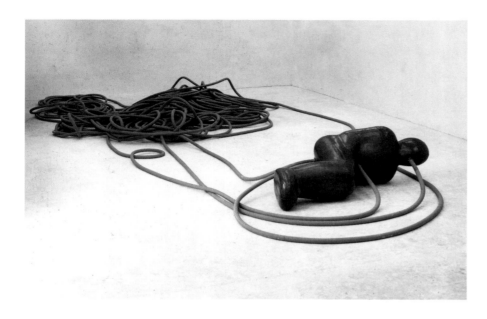

Sovereign State 1989/90

mouth to the anus, and the penis to the navel, and now in this installation we're going to have one room full of these pipes and in the other the astronaut-like expanded piece. The pipes will be heaped on the floor, like a telephone exchange in a crisis.

But the body itself is quite muddled, isn't it?

No, the body is the way it is. The mind is muddled. One's first relationship is with one's body. Then through one's body one begins to build up another kind of constellation of affection and, hopefully, an emerging sense of some kind of purpose. The sense of emerging purpose that a family describes has to be re-possessed as one of the points of resistance against the dispersal of self in consumer values.

You constantly use an image of another kind of dispersal in your discussion of the work, from individual pieces using lead, to the collective in 'Field', and now to the new iron work which is made up of several pieces.

I'm thinking of calling the work 'Testing a World View' (pp 104–7). The work is a kind of psychological Cubism. An identical body cast made from the interior of a body case five times, which I then try to test against architecture. The piece expresses the polymorphousness of the self; that in different places we become different and I think this is physical. If Cubism is about taking one object and making multiple views of it in one place, this is a dispersion of one object into several cases for itself.

Laocoön

Does it always have to be your own body?

I want to confront existence. It is obviously going to mean more if I use my own body. The optical and the conceptual have dominated in the art of the twentieth century and I turn to the body in an attempt to find a language that will transcend the limitations of race, creed and language, but which will still be about the rootedness of identity. It isn't just an idea about finding an idiom that could be universal, in a way that Modernism failed to do, it is an invitation to recognise a place and a base of consciousness. The body – I keep coming to this idea – is a moving sensor. I want the body to be a sensing mechanism, so your response to the work does not have to be pre-informed and does not necessarily encourage discourse. We are taught to use vision as an identifying force, which allied to discriminating intelligence fixes a thing. So that the strategy, for example, of Richard Deacon, deconstructing the physical world by suggesting multiple readings and denying any one in particular, is one possible strategy. But if you believe in subjects, which I do, you have to find another way. If my subject is being, somehow I have to manage to engage the whole *being* of the viewer.

I have always been bothered with the idea that the most visible bits of the Western figurative tradition of sculpture are dramatic muscular actions made in marble or bronze like the 'Discobolus', the 'Laocoön', or that fantastic Bernini work, 'David'. What it suggests is that human potential can only be expressed sculpturally through the depiction of

Kroissos c 525 BC

Michelangelo *Slave* 1516–20

action. That moment of placing one foot in front of the other which began with the archaic Kouroi and continues with Michaelangelo's 'Slaves', suggests that muscular action expresses the metaphysical tension between spirit and body, but I'm not so sure. Rodin momentarily recovered from that trap with his 'Age of Bronze'; presenting a moment of becoming. What started as a heroic image of the soldier ends up being internalised and becomes a moment of self-consciousness within the body. For me this reconnects with the timelessness of pre-archaic Cycladic Greek sculpture which obviously uses the body in a completely different way as presence rather than actor. The head always addresses itself to the sky. There is something very powerful about the way that both Rodin's 'Age of Bronze', and the Cycladic heads connect being with the infinity of the sky, suggesting human potential, but not in terms of movement. I want to recapture that sense of imaginative space inside the body. I want there to be an internal pressure in the work, that has a relationship with the atmosphere which we sense with our bodies through the skin of the work.

How else do you engage the viewer?

Through scale; 'Field' makes the viewer feel big, and the expansion pieces make one feel rather small. Playing on scale (which is not the same as size) makes us feel our bodies-in-the-world.

How does that work with the concrete pieces?

Idol from Amorgos 2500–1100 BC

Rodin *The Age of Bronze* 1875–6

The block describes the space between the body and a compressed notion of architecture, and what I find makes them quite tender is that the principle gesture of all those works is touch. Materiality in sculpture invites touch. They don't. The body that touches is not there and what is touched is space, engaging the air. The concrete has become, as it were, a necessary conditionality. The work has always identified the minimum space necessary for a man to occupy but I think the concrete pieces do it in a more intimate, open and direct way. There is a real point of contact with the particularity of my body – slipped from life into art, with every wrinkle of the knuckles embedded in the concrete. Maybe the concrete works have found a new way of engaging with the central premises of western sculpture: the relationship of idea to raw materials, image to block.

Are you trying to articulate the silence of the minimal cube?

I think there are other kinds of silence, which are different from the silence of formal certainty, and which can encourage subjective response.

Judd has very powerfully mapped out an absolute in the physical and theoretical territory of his work. It's interesting that Jefferson mapped the Western states of the United States as a grid, as absolutes, and then sent the explorers Lewis and Clark to confirm them. Conception came before perception and demanded a complete invalidation of what and who was there originally and their relationship with the territory. Dominant forces simply do not recognise the 'other' and in that sense neither does puritanical Modernism.

In 'Field', the earth is being allowed to carry the voice of the other to re-affirm the spirit of the land that lives through the people. The American 'Field' has a strong presence of the original inhabitants of that continent. This is distinct from the pioneers' dreams of possession of the land, where a map is conceptualised ground. I want to make the ground fruitful for the mind. The grid you have drawn – that imposes on the land – is distinct from the aboriginal intuition which is one of human consciousness being a *continuation* of the land, the feeling that they are embedded in the land, which is to do with the continuum between human and mineral life.

There is a distinction here between the idea of living and the idea of being lived. Aboriginal cultures across the world have different concepts of possession of the land. Since there now seems to be a terminal sense to nineteenth century expansive Capitalism – of which Modernism is a product – different possibilities must exist for collaborative relationships, such as those involved in making a work like 'Field', in Mexico, and then the making and showing of it elsewhere, as you have done in Malmö, and will do in St. Helens.

There are lots of things to talk about here, but for me, one of the most important things is that through sharing the engendering of the work, the makers are also the work's first audience and it is not like the audience of a spectacle. It's more like a collective experience of active imaginative involvement. I am inviting a group of people to spend some time with the earth in a way that they wouldn't normally do, to touch it again and again. There is a ritual which is important. We work on the floor at the level of the work.

Could you call it harvesting?

It is a kind of harvesting – it's about tilling the earth with your hands but instead of making something grow, it is the earth you are forming directly. The harvest comes from within the people, or the thing that is growing comes out of the people. Everyone has their own row and throughout the project they continue to do row after row on the same strip like the old medieval strip field and they build up a very strong relationship with that patch of earth. Those gazes that they are seeding in the clay look back at them as they are working, suggesting that consciousness is not only inside. I see it as a kind of soul garden. It is a fragile thing but it is a link – both personal to the person who is making them and also common to all of us – something to do with the way in which the figures house the memory. That memory is transpersonal and yet we all have a personal relationship with the future. For me, 'Field' is the consummation of being the other, a kind of liberation in many ways – *of* many ways.

August 1993

Field 1991

The Raising of Lazarus
Stephen Bann

Sometimes it is said today that the work of contemporary artists has completely taken leave of the issues that concerned their predecessors in the Western tradition. It is as if we needed one pair of eyes to look at the achievements of a medieval, or Renaissance master, and quite a new pair to look at (and make sense of) the work produced by an artist of our own time. My own impression is that the situation is a little more complicated than that. Certainly it is true that we can develop stereotyped ways of seeing, which appear to fit the works of the illustrious past and cannot accommodate those of the present. But the genuinely creative approach renews the appeal of the past artist at the same time as it engages with the challenge of the contemporary period. It is a commonplace that, at the turn of the century, critics and connoisseurs rediscovered the forgotten Piero della Francesca at the same time (and, we might say, with the same eyes) as they were engaging with Cézanne.

Our own period is no exception to this rule. It is true, of course, that Modernism, with its concomitant abstraction, seemed to put a full stop after the many centuries of figurative art, and propose a completely new starting point for the visual artist. But what the modernist impulse turns out to have destroyed is not tradition, or figurative art, but a certain way of reading the tradition of figuration: one that Norman Bryson has described in terms of the myth of the 'essential copy'[1]. What has been destroyed, in other words, is a particular way of interpreting the mimetic role of the work of art, its status as a 'copy' of elements in the external world. Surfeited as we are with the new technologies of photography, film and television (not to mention 'virtual reality'), we can no longer accept the crude principle which has nonetheless been refined by countless critics and commentators over the centuries: that the excellence of a work of art depends on the degree of perfection with which it succeeds in simulating a referent in the 'real' world.

But a new, and vital, question arises at this point. If we throw out mimesis – the 'essential copy' – then what remains? It may no longer be credible to hold, as Ruskin did in some respects, that art is a long and arduous ascent to the point where technique is finally adequate to capture the superlative grandeur of the natural world. But abandoning this evolutionary theory does not imply dismissing altogether the continuous, if problematic link between the images of art and the forms of the external world, which is based not solely on technique but on the operation of religious or magical connections.

A recent and influential work by David Freedberg, aptly titled *The Power of Images*, makes this point very forcibly. In one of his opening chapters, he quotes a fascinating passage from the work of the contemporary German philosopher, Hans-Georg Gadamer:

> ... if it is only at the beginning of the history of the picture, in its prehistory as it were, that we find picture magic, which depends on the identity and non-differentiation of picture and what is pictured, still this does not mean that an increasingly differentiated consciousness of the picture that grows further and further away from magical identity can ever detach itself entirely from it. Rather, non-differentiation remains an essential feature of all experience of pictures ... [2].

Put simply, this means that the process of 'copying' the external world is not something that outgrows its primitive, magical origins, or becomes displaced on to the primarily technical pursuit of an 'essential copy'. The picture (and here of course Gadamer's point also applies *a fortiori* to the three-dimensional realisations of sculpture) cannot throw off its inheritance of 'magical identity', that is, the condition in which it manifests directly the power of what it presents. Clearly this is a feature above all of religious art, and Gadamer is categorical in stating that religious art, in this respect, is not an aberrant category but the 'exemplary' instance for the whole 'picture-making' tradition: 'In it we can see without doubt that a picture is not a copy of a copied being, but is in ontological communion with what is copied'.

In beginning this essay on Antony Gormley in this way, I intend not to divert attention from its contemporary validity, but to indicate, on the contrary, the multiple processes of re-interpretation which help to account for the timeliness, and rightness, of a particular means of expression. What I am arguing is that Gormley's development as a sculptor over the last two decades is not merely an autonomous process, which can be traced through a sequence of characteristic themes and a gradual evolution of techniques. It has been a process of understanding, and that understanding has been a measure both of his participation in the current, complex revaluation of the Western tradition, and in the

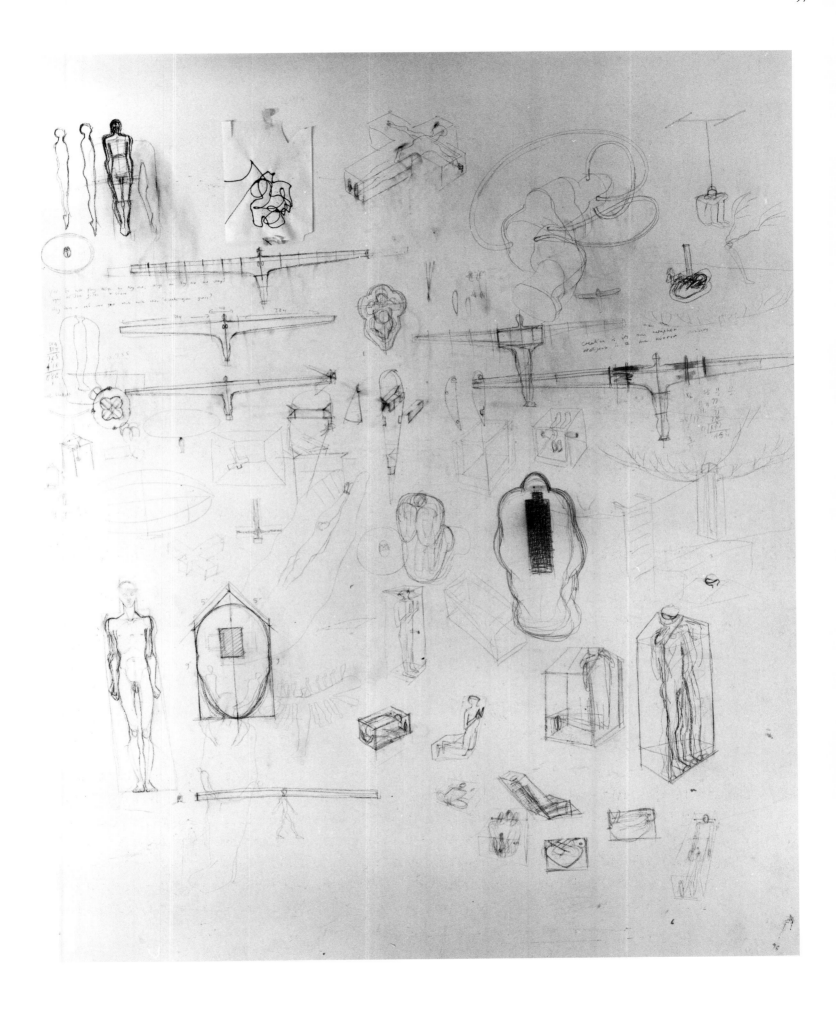

Studio wall 1993

more recent history of a Modernism that has turned itself inside out, so to speak, in the fulfilment of its own logic. The works grouped together in this exhibition are therefore, on one level, an extraordinarily convincing demonstration of how to extricate oneself from Modernism without (one might say) breaking the mould[3]. But they are also compelling instances of the proposition that artists, too, are engaged in fundamental intellectual research: their mode may be governed by the special, intrinsic law of form, but their insights rejoin at a more basic level the combined insights of the critics, historians and philosophical thinkers who are engaged, in their own domains, with re-interpretating the world in which we live[4].

I want to dismiss straight away, however, any impression that my emphasis on 'religious' or 'magical' properties (as defined by Gadamer) would imply a sentimental reconciliation with outworn and exhausted habits of thought. 'Religious art', as it is made today, almost invariably turns out to be a pastiche of some earlier style or manner, and hence no art at all. But this does not stop contemporary art of the highest quality recalling the 'magical' or 'religious' precisely in the domain to which Gadamer draws attention: that of the feature of 'non-differentiation'. Antony Gormley's 'Sound II', 1986 recently installed in the sometimes flooded crypt of Winchester Cathedral, creates an unforgettable effect of presence. It is not an image with a traditional iconographic reading. In fact, like all of Gormley's recent sculpture, it is the product of a cast taken from the artist's own body, which is given its own identity through a particular choice of attitude and gesture. But if it is not 'religious art' in the sense of representing a particular saint or prophet, it partakes of the 'non-differentiation' signalled by Gadamer. In the reduced light of the crypt, the specific technical features of Gormley's work – the dull glow emitted by the sheets of lead and the fidelity of bodily reference ensured by the casting process – produce a subtly commingled effect. We see a figure which is both distanced and near, produced by a technical process which is amply evident from the soldered joints between the lead sheets, and yet imposing itself as a presence in the vaulted space. Semiologists have an exact way of expressing the perceptible difference from traditional concepts of representation which this effect implies. The figure is not only an 'icon' – hence related to its referent by a simple relation of resemblance – but also an 'index' – related by direct contiguity in such a way that, like a death-mask or a footprint, it remains a material trace of its referent. This is a feature which is not just incidental, but helps to determine our whole attitude of viewing.

Sound II 1986 (Winchester Cathedral)

Jacob Epstein *Lazarus* 1947–8

Such an achievement can, by its very aptness, help us to see other configurations of work and context in a new and fresh way. My first acquaintance with Epstein's sculpture of 'Lazarus', 1947–8 installed in the retro-choir of New College Chapel, Oxford, was not a particularly happy one, as I missed the intense lighting of the modern museum and was puzzled at the grey pallor cast over the figure of the resurrected Lazarus as he struggles to free himself from the toils of his linen winding sheet. Gormley's work helps me to reinterpret not only the context in which 'Lazarus' is placed, but also the strange and compelling tension with which Epstein has invested it, on the sculptural level. Of course the work is carved in stone. But something of Epstein's ambivalence – as a carver of egregiously modernist icons and as a modeller of naturalistic clay busts – seems to come through in the very representation of the laborious spiral movement. A body seems to force itself from within, so that the formal patterning of the stone folds appears ready to flake away in response to it.

Lazarus is indeed a precedent to bear in mind when looking at Gormley's sculpture, since the image of the decayed body brought suddenly back to life conflicts so decisively with the ideal, heroic tradition of sculpture which we derive from the Greeks. For obvious reasons, we associate the representation of Lazarus more closely with the pictorial

Sebastiano del Piombo *The Raising of Lazarus* 1517–9

Michelangelo *Rondanini Pieta*

than with the sculptural mode. But even in paintings, the enigma of the resurrected body of Lazarus has given rise to fascinating speculations on the representational status of such a body, which seems to elude the conventional economy of mimesis. The English critic William Hazlitt writes about Sebastiano del Piombo's great painting 'The Raising of Lazarus', 1517–9: 'The Lazarus is very fine and bold. The flesh is well-baked, dingy and ready to crumble from the touch, when it is liberated from its dread confinement to have life and motion impressed upon it again'[5]. Hazlitt is appealing to the vivid evidence of the senses – the sense of touch in particular – in order to conjure up the plastic effect of a body represented in an extreme condition of paradox, both 'well-baked' and instinct with lively motion. It is an effect strangely parallel to that of Gormley's lead-coated sculpture, where the 'baking' of the molten material never distances the body so far as to erase the impulse of life. We might easily extend this point to take into account the whole issue of the representation of the dead – but revivified – body in the Western tradition. Sebastiano del Piombo's master, Michelangelo, developed to a hitherto inconceivable extent the powerful implications of the dead body as icon. In a late work like the 'Rondanini Pieta', the figure of Christ is an inert mass following the forces of gravity. But as its heaviness draws it down to the earth, its symbolic power invests it with energy, and produces a reverse, upward movement which we can interpret as the burgeoning of the life force.

Close I 1992

The installation of a work like 'Sound II' in a religious building encourages this train of comparisons, impelling us to a re-reading of Epstein's modernist sculpture at the same time as it refreshes our perception of Renaissance masters. But it should be emphasised that it is not the context, however inspired it may be, that enables Gormley's sculpture to function in this way. On the contrary, these works can irradiate the neutral, apparently context-free spaces of the modern gallery, in such a way that a similar experience takes place. 'Close I', 1992 for example, spreads the human body into four diagonal, linear impulses which extend its energy across the flat floor surface: lead tends, however slowly, to 'creep' in accordance with the law of gravity as a result of its considerable weight, and this state of the sculptural body seems to reconcile an entropic and an energetic motion. 'A Case for an Angel II', 1990 extends the body laterally in two dimensions, and contrasts the contained nucleus of the body with the beaten lead 'wings' which offer it buoyancy and equilibrium. (In the context of the exhibition, 'Vehicle', 1987 likewise appears as an extrapolation of bodily impulses and properties to the domain of the expanded space). It is noteworthy that in the technical description of these pieces Gormley does not stop at declaring the medium to be lead – the external carapace which meets the eye – but also specifies the materials lying beneath the surface: in the case of 'Close I', glass fibre, plaster... and air. 'Sound II' is filled with water, 'Close I' with air. The elements flow in and out of the sculptures just as, through transpiration and respiration, they flow in and out of ourselves.

There is, however, a reference point in recent art which has to be taken into account,

A Case for an Angel II 1990

before we can fully appreciate the dynamic relationship which Gormley establishes between the work and its spatial context. Looking at the way in which he distributes a sequence of solid iron body forms holding 90° angles, placed in different positions across the room (pp 104–7), we might well find a memory stirring of a similarly resourceful animation of the gallery environment – and we might be surprised to realise that we were thinking of one of Robert Morris' minimalist installations of identical metal units (p 65). In the case of the Gormley work, we would notice the particular effect of muscular tension implicit in the bodily posture of these sculptural figures, variously configured in relation to floor and walls. But the strategy would still seem comparable, not to say directly related. That this is not just a random association, or a purely formal comparison, seems to me to require some justification. And this can be found in the recent revaluation of the whole phenomenon of Minimalism which has been provided by the French critic and art historian, Georges Didi-Huberman.

In 1992, Didi-Huberman published two complementary studies of contemporary sculpture, both concerned with the inadequacy of prevalent distinctions between 'abstraction' and 'figuration'. The first, *Le Cube et le visage* (*The Cube and the face*), addressed itself to a single enigmatic work by Alberto Giacometti, 'The Cube', 1934. The second, with the evocative title *Ce que nous voyons, ce qui nous regarde* (*What we see, what looks at us*)[6], looked at the development of minimalist sculpture from the 1960s onwards in the light of Walter Benjamin's notion of 'aura', and Michael Fried's well-known distinction between art and 'theatricality'[7].

Tony Smith *Die* 1962   Fra Angelico *The Last Judgement* (detail)

Although the detail of Didi-Huberman's argument cannot be reproduced here, the message which emerges from both studies is unequivocal, and highly relevant to the work under consideration here. It is as if he were rescuing the whole notion of 'abstraction' from a kind of prohibition which it had been forced to undergo, as the most distinctive, pace-setting mode of modernist art. Where Benjamin proclaims the loss of 'aura' in the 'age of mechanical reproduction', and Fried attacks the 'theatricality' with which minimalist sculpture places itself across the path of the spectator, Didi-Huberman sees both positions as attempts to deny an incontrovertible fact: that abstract sculpture does indeed have presence, and that it is a presence derived from our sense of another body which mysteriously, yet uncompromisingly, stands in our way. Michael Fried was right, in other words, to compare the aesthetic effect of 'theatricality' which, as a modernist, he so detested, to the sense of being invaded by the silent presence of another person. But Didi-Huberman treats this phenomenon not as a radical defect, but as an affirmation of the continuity of an artistic tradition which is, in its origin, inescapably religious: he illustrates next to Tony Smith's 'Die', 1962 and Donald Judd's hollow cubes, the empty tombs of Fra Angelico's 'The Last Judgement'.

It is not at all necessary to assert that Didi-Huberman's reading of Minimalism is 'right', whilst the official position both of its protagonists and its assailants (like Fried) must be classed as 'wrong'. Certainly the declared aim of the minimalists was to expel every vestige of anthropomorphism. But equally certainly, the character of their work (and of some of their early writings) betokens a recognition of the dyadic nature of the act of

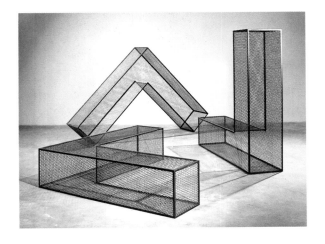

Robert Morris *The Ells* 1965–88   Carl André *Equivalent VIII* 1966

seeing: 'what we see' is also 'what looks at us'. No one who has experienced the effect of one of the outstanding minimalist installations – for example, 'Weight and Measure', the two-part work installed by Richard Serra in the axial galleries of the Tate Gallery in 1992 – can deny that their occupancy of space is incomparably more powerful than a reductive reading of their elements would lead one to suppose. And it is not necessary to rely simply on the experience of spectators to substantiate this point. The unequivocal evidence of the development of a sculptor like Antony Gormley is there as well.

For the current exhibition demonstrates beyond a doubt that, for Gormley, the example of Minimalism proved to be serviceable in a way which indirectly supports Didi-Huberman's analysis. He is not of course unique in this respect: sculptors as diverse in their achievements as Robert Gober, in America, Pascal Convert, in France, and Stephen Cox, in Britain, have all worked from a basis in minimalist sculpture to a preoccupation with the human figure, without abandoning the resourceful use of space which characterised the minimalist sculptors. But Gormley is certainly one of the artists who has retained at the deepest level the sense that Minimalism was not a rupture in the sculptural tradition, but a reinforcement of its deepest continuities. One of his earliest significant works, 'Bed', 1980–1 (p 16) can in fact be seen as a revision of the notorious 'Equivalent VIII', 1966 by Carl André, which stirred up controversy some years after its entry into the collection of the Tate Gallery. It is not simply that Gormley replaces the standardised bricks with industrially produced bread, and leaves the imprint of his body on the horizontal surface. This could be seen as a directly contestatory gesture, whereas in fact

Sense 1991

Gormley has emphasised that the relationship involves a kind of revaluation of the work by André, which is itself also a base, and could be thought of as a kind of bed or table. The new work therefore does not reject, but more exactly recuperates its predecessor: in a sense, it humanises retrospectively a work which had suffered, and was still to suffer, from the effects of a particularly arid artistic controversy.

Gormley's continuing and productive engagement with the minimalist example is, as I have said, demonstrated by the evidence of this exhibition. I spoke at the outset of Modernism turning itself inside out, and this does seem to me a more effective way of looking at the current period than is warranted by the permissive philosophy of Post-Modernism. For an art like that of Gormley does not just declare itself emancipated from the modernist legacy, and free to invoke any and every cultural precedent. It reinterprets the past from the inside, so to speak. Whether we locate as our basis of continuity the 'non-differentiation' between the work and the referent noted by Gadamer, or the implicit human presence in the most 'abstract' of containers, we can collect evidence not only from the writings of critics and philosophers, but from the particular forms which Gormley's work has come to adopt.

These comments apply especially to the recent sculptures which, together with the lead and iron body cases already mentioned, make up the major part of the exhibition. The cast concrete pieces, with their abstract forms, and smooth surfaces infringed only by the

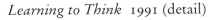
Learning to Think 1991 (detail)   Marcel Duchamp *The Large Glass* 1915–23 (detail)

external sign of a body part breaking through to the outside edge, are surely inescapable metaphors for the implicit human presence in the minimal form. We can find out about the technical procedure which the artist followed: in this case, the production of a wax cast from his own body which is 'lost' (by the traditional *cire perdu* technique) within the concrete mould. But this does not alter the fact that the indexical presence of that 'lost body' must be sensed by the spectator: it must be reconstituted, by a process which we cannot really call 'conceptual'. To put it another way, we know that the geometrical form contains, in its hollow interior, the imprint of a body. But at the same time, we see, through the very index of the hand or head that breaks the surface, the impenetrable inner space that forms the negative of that body. What seems to be called for is an act of empathy, or trust, to which the work convokes us. I am reminded of Verrocchio's 'Christ and St Thomas', on the facade of Orsanmichele in Florence, where the sculptor has shown the moment of the apostle responding to Christ's invitation, and putting his hand in the open wound. In a certain way, Antony Gormley's concrete pieces also stage, for the adventurous or doubting spectator, a drama of the mystery of incarnation.

One of the significant effects of a concrete piece like 'Sense', 1991, in the context of this exhibition, is to remind us that even Gormley's lead sculptures were never, in a tradition-al sense, iconic. The generalisation of bodily features by the properties of the lead sheet-ing, and the evident soldering of the joints, always distanced them from the illusionistic mode of neo-classical sculpture, while stressing the indexical link with a particular, rather than an ideal body: these were (and are) moulds, in some ways akin to the leaden 'Malic Moulds' with which Duchamp invests his bachelors in 'The Large Glass', 1915–23, but of course jettisoning Duchamp's ironic distance in favour of an absolute authorial identification. In the further series of 'expanded' works which are featured in this exhibition, the limits of indexical reference – indeed the limits of any bodily identification – are even more strenuously tested. A work like 'Still Running', 1990/3 suggests an obvious modernist pedigree. We might think of the ability of a sculptor like Jean Arp to devise concrete forms which relate at the same time to the animal and the vegetative world: these connotations of the fruit ripening, or the seed burgeoning, are certainly not out of place in considering these large iron casts, whose free-floating poise is sometimes emphasised by them being suspended from the ceiling. Yet once again Gormley is working on the transformations of the body, which remains, quite literally, at the unseen core of the sculptural form. By a systematic process which is analogous to the traditional 'pointing' of plaster casts for reproduction, he establishes a network of lines which sprout from the body cast, and establish surfaces whose relation to the original figure can sometimes be deduced by the spectator. Gormley's concern, however, is not with the legibility of the figure, but with moving beyond the barrier of appearance, and posing questions about our place in the created world.

This concern to avoid any element of formalism in his representation of the body, which is evident in the whole range of work displayed here, finds perhaps its most striking expression in the remarkable installation entitled 'Field' (pp 100–4). In this case, Gormley has filled an entire room with tiny clay figurines whose common characteristic is their intently staring gaze. (At the original installation of the work at Salvatore Ala Gallery, New York in 1989, the number of figurines was only 150, but by 1991, at a later showing, the total had increased to 35,000, made in conjunction with a family of brickmakers in Cholula, Mexico. The two versions shown in this exhibition are again collaborative ventures. 'European Field', shown in Malmö was made in Östra Grevie, Sweden; 'Field for the British Isles', shown in Liverpool and Dublin, was made in St Helens, England). No more eloquent demonstration could be imagined of the dialectical nature of the act of seeing, and of the truth embodied in the title of Didi-Huberman's book: What we see [is] what looks at us. But it would be wrong to present this work as in any sense the demonstration of an abstract theory for its own sake, when the logic of its presentation is so clearly embedded both in the tradition of modernist sculpture and in the development of Gormley's own career as a sculptor. On the one hand, 'Field' can be viewed as the con-

Still Running 1990/3 (plaster)

clusive disinvestment of the sculptor in his own body image, and the achievement of a dimension of otherness which is not only technical (the collaborative element) but (one might say) existential. We as spectators become the focus of a gaze which is firm and inflexible, without being menacing. On the other hand, it is a work which does not disavow its deep connections with a prior tradition involving Duchamp's last work, the 'Etant donnés', where the spectator views the *tableau vivant* through a peep-hole and becomes conscious of the libidinal economy implied in seeing and being seen. Viewing 'Field' from outside the doorway which frames it seems a voyeuristic experience, at the first level; but it can also be experienced as the coming into being of a new type of relationship with the world of representation. It is as if the proscenium arch had been turned round, and we ourselves were on stage, confronted by a myriad of viewers[8].

In a thoughtful essay on one of the presentations of 'Field', Thomas McEvilley used the evocative title, *Seeds of the Future*. It is impossible, in effect, not to take account of the pervasive Utopian character of all of Antony Gormley's work, which is entirely consistent with his need to revise and reinterpret, rather than abjure, the great collective experi-

Field 1991

ment of Modernism. Thinking of his development against the context of the Western tradition as a whole, I am reminded of the reiterated images of the Last Judgement which crowd the facades of so many European abbeys and cathedrals. Each represents a definitive demarcation, literally a 'judgement', between the bodies of the damned which descend to Hell and the glorified bodies which are gathered up into Paradise. In the same way, the bodies of Gormley's sculpture – the innumberable figurines of 'Field' and 'Sound II' in its cathedral crypt – seem to be transfixed in waiting: not because they expect some imminent and irreversible decree, but as if their glorification depended uniquely on us.

Notes

1. See Norman Bryson, *Vision and Painting – The Logic of the Gaze*, London, 1983, pp 6–35; the issue of the 'essential copy' is also discussed in my own study, *The True Vine – On Visual Representation and the Western Tradition*, Cambridge, 1989, p 27 ff.

2. Quoted in David Freedberg, *The Power of Images: Studies in the History and Theory of Response*, London, 1989, p 77. Freedberg ranges widely over the many forms that have been customarily excluded from serious discussion by art historians, such as votive images, waxworks and erotica, in order to show how arbitrary a line has been drawn between 'aesthetic' and other forms of response.

3. A striking confirmation of Gormley's dialectical attitude to the formulations of Modernist orthodoxy can be found in the following observation. He writes: 'If late modernist painting conflated the figure and the ground in the interests of a single unequivocal surface, I propose that the body is the ground and that at the other side of appearance is a space far greater than the space against which, traditionally, the body is figured. If Caspar David Friedrich's 'Monk and the Sea' is a Rothko with a man in it, I am trying to make a case for a man containing the boundless space of consciousness' (*Antony Gormley*, Contemporary Sculpture Center, Tokyo, 1992, unpaginated). Another way of putting this is to say that Modernism implied a diffusion of the figure in the field, whilst Gormley attempts to identify the field inside the figure. The 'sublime' dimension which a Northern Romantic painter like Friedrich displaces on to the landscape is relocated in consciousness. The artist's task is to organise the conditions under which that internal consciousness becomes accessible to perception.

4. This profound symmetry between the work of the artist and that of the thinker can often be masked by the fact that second-hand theories become diffused through our culture, and acquire the force of orthodoxy (what Roland Barthes would have called doxa) precisely at the time when their authors have largely abandoned them and turned in another direction. It is amusing to note that Umberto Eco's theory of the 'open work', which developed in the 1960s, has been used to justify a kind of post-modern eclecticism. Eco, however, has in recent years become preoccupied with defining the limits of interpretation, and with tracing broad patterns of historical continuity, as in his study of the search for the 'perfect language'. It goes without saying that Antony Gormley's strategy has more in common with Eco's recent work than with the earlier phase.

5. Hazlitt, *Complete Works*, London, 1930–4, vol x, pp 10–11.

6. See Georges Didi-Huberman, *Le Cube et le Visage – Autour d'une sculpture d'Alberto Giacometti*, Paris, 1992, and *Ce que nous voyons, ce qui nous regarde*, Paris, 1992. Didi-Huberman notes that Rosalind Krauss was right to put the names of Rodin and Brancusi at the very centre of her study of minimalist sculpture; his discussion of the remarkable 'The Cube' by Giacometti proceeds from the assumption that its 'extreme formalism *gave rise* to the very question of the portrait, which was put from the basis of an absence, of a humanity by default' (*Ce que nous voyons*, p 102).

7. Michael Fried, 'Art and Objecthood' in *Art in Theory*, ed. Charles Harrison and Paul Wood, Oxford, 1992, pp 822–33.

8. Gormley himself sees a precedent in Piero Manzoni's 'Socle du Monde' for this work which consists in 'looking to the life that is looking at it'.

Plates

Instrument 1988/93 and *Exposure* 1988/93

Body and Light 1988/93 and *Meaning* 1988/93

Augur 1989/93 and *Oracle* 1989/93

Bridge 1993 and *Centre* 1993

Immersion 1991

Sense 1991

Flesh 1990

Home of the Heart III 1992

Home of the Heart II 1993

Home of the Heart I 1993

Earth, Fruit, Body, all 1991/93 (Malmö Konsthall)

Fruit 1991/3

End Product 1990/3

Earth 1991/3

Body 1991/3

Still Running 1990/3

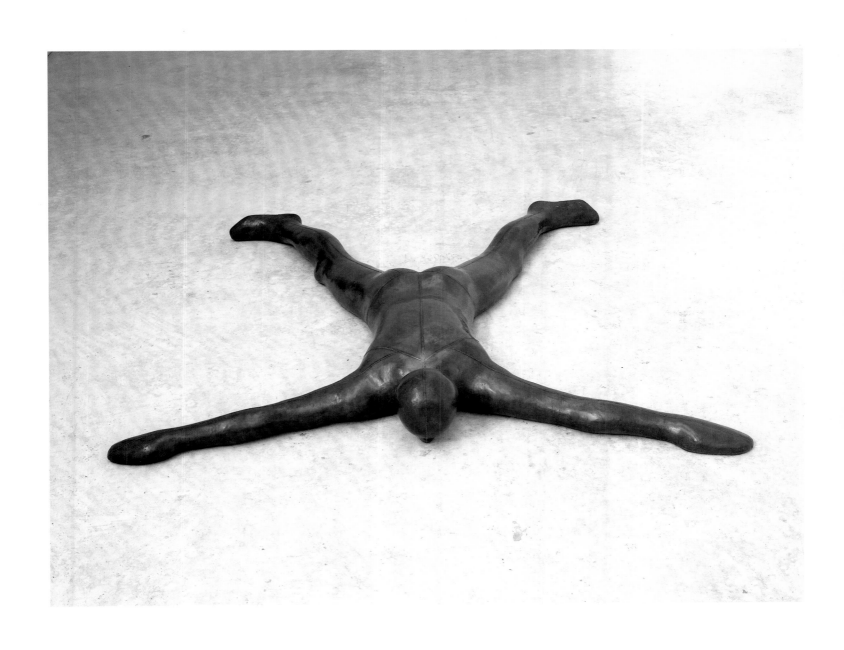

Close I 1992

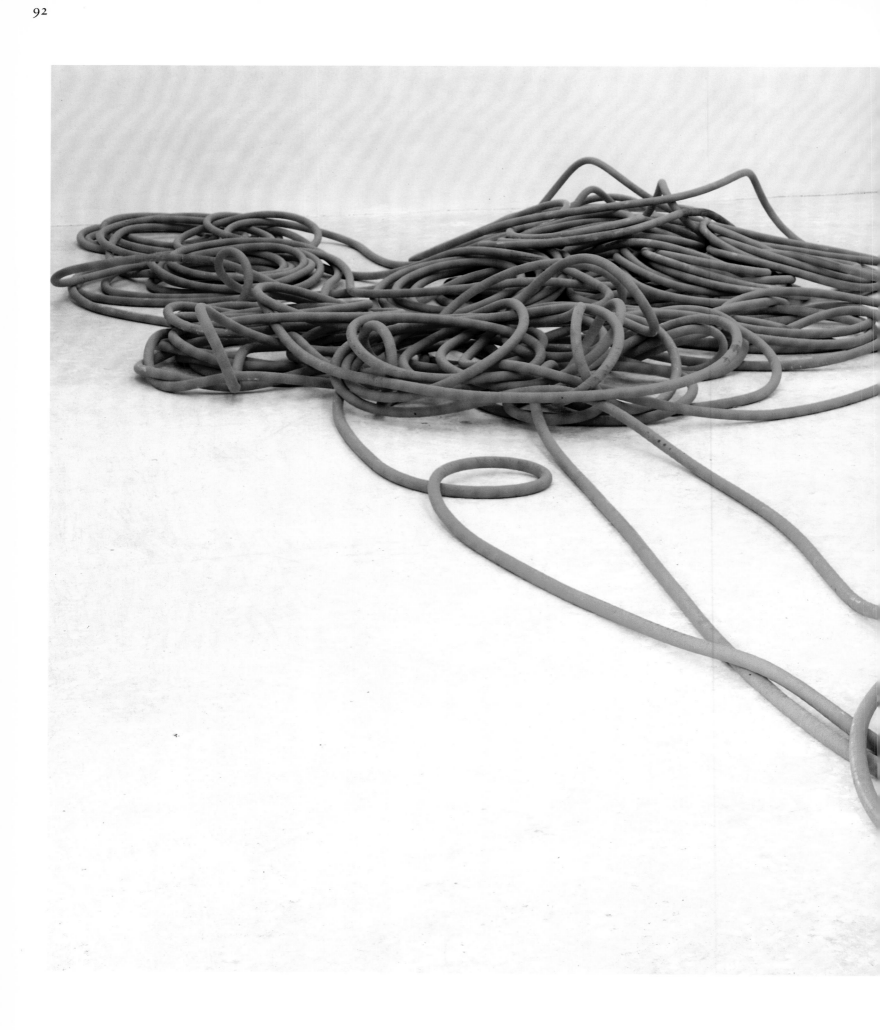

Sovereign State 1989/90

Seeing and Showing 1991/2

Bearing 1987/93

Vehicle 1987

A Case for an Angel II 1990

A Case for an Angel III 1990

European Field 1993 (Malmö Konsthall)

European Field 1993

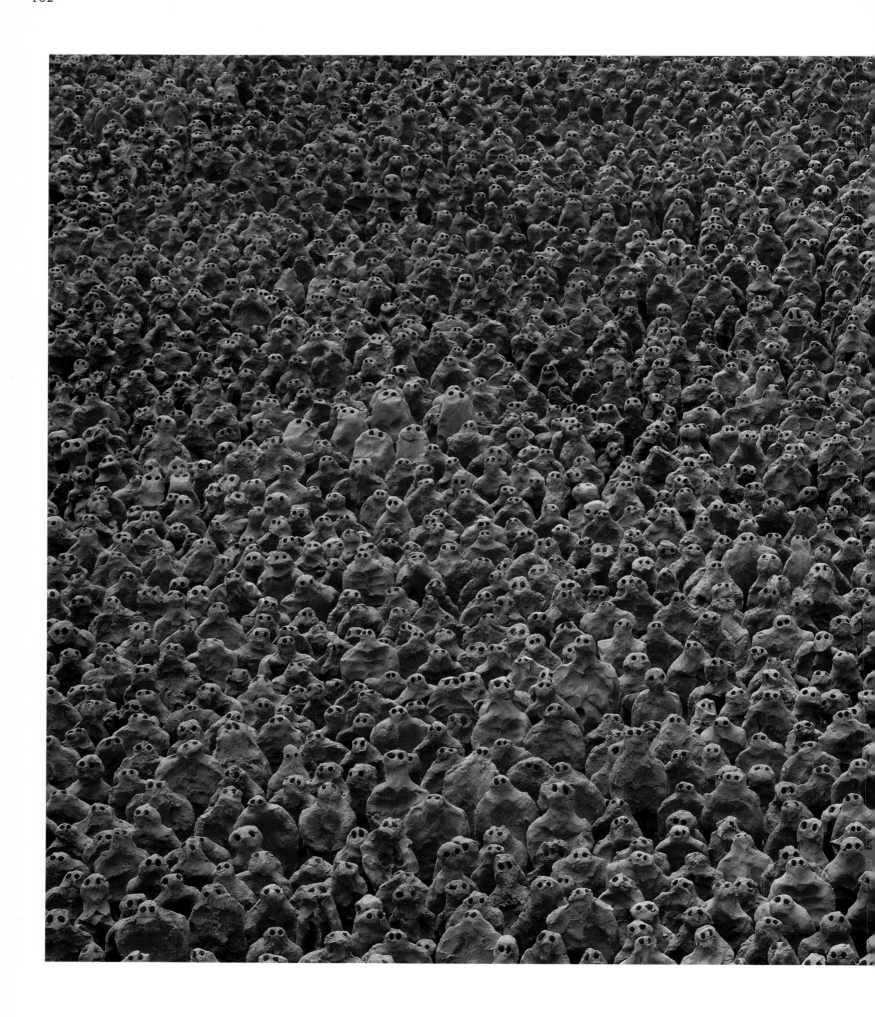

European Field 1993 (detail)

Testing a World View 1993 (detail)

Testing a World View 1993 (with *Seeds V*, 1989/93)

Testing a World View 1993 (Malmö Konsthall)

List of Illustrations

Dimensions: height followed by width and depth in millimetres
Unless stated otherwise, works are in the collection of the artist
* denotes work in exhibition

Sleeping Place 1974
Plaster, linen
600 x 760 x 1520 (p 12)
(destroyed)

Open Door 1975
Wooden door
2060 x 2060 (p 13)
Private Collection, London

Land, Sea and Air I 1977–9
Lead, stone, water, air
Each unit approx 200 x 310 x 20 (p 17)
Private Collection, London

Fruits of the Earth 1978–9
Lead, revolver, bottle, machete, wine
Largest element approx 600 long (p 14)
Private Collection, London

Last Tree 1979
Cedar wood
250 x 850 (p 15)

Exercise Between Blood and Earth 1979/81
Chalk on wall
1840 diam (pp 17, 29)
(destroyed)

Room 1980
Socks, shoes, pants, trousers, shirt, pullover, vest, jacket
1570 x 7000 x 7000 (p 18)

Bed 1980–1
Bread, wax
280 x 2200 x 1680 (p 16)
Private Collection, London

Three Ways; Mould, Hole and Passage 1981
Lead, fibreglass, plaster
Mould: 600 x 980 x 500;
Hole: 620 x 1230 x 800;
Passage: 340 x 2090 x 500 (p 19)
Private Collection, London

Natural Selection 1981
Lead, tools, fruits, weapons, vegetables, objects
Largest unit 200 diam
Length approx 10 metres (p 14)

Land, Sea and Air II 1982
Lead, fibreglass
Land (crouching): 450 x 1030 x 50;
Sea (standing): 1910 x 500 x 320;
Air (kneeling): 1180 x 690 x 520 (p 21)
Collection of Samuel and Ronnie Heyman

Peer 1984
Lead, plaster, fibreglass
1880 x 500 x 430 (p 24)
Courtesy Salvatore Ala Gallery, New York

Sound II 1986
Lead, fibreglass, water
1880 x 600 x 450 (p 59)
Dean and Chapter, Winchester Cathedral

Vehicle 1987 *
Lead, fibreglass, wood, steel, air
1470 x 7500 x 15200 (p 24, 96–7)
Courtesy Salvatore Ala Gallery, New York
(Tate Gallery Liverpool)

Room II 1987
Concrete
2080 x 510 x 660 (p 27)
Courtesy Salvatore Ala Gallery, New York

The Brick Man (Model) 1987
Terracotta, fibreglass, plaster
1960 x 500 x 380 (p 31)
Leeds City Art Galleries

Bearing 1987/93 *
Lead, fibreglass, plaster, air
2450 x 980 x 830 (p 95)
(Tate Gallery Liverpool)

Instrument 1988/93 *
Lead, fibreglass
305 x 305 x 305 (pp 25, 74)
Courtesy Galerie Nordenhake, Sweden

Exposure 1988/93 *
Lead, fibreglass, air, alabaster
330 x 305 x 305, 2 eggs/testicles each 50 long, 33 diam (pp 25, 74)
Courtesy Galerie Nordenhake, Sweden

Body and Light 1988/93 *
Lead, fibreglass, air, resin
380 x 305 x 305, brain 90 x 130 x 160 (p 75)
Courtesy Galerie Nordenhake, Sweden

Meaning 1988/93 *
Lead, fibreglass
305 x 305 x 305 (p 75)
Courtesy Galerie Nordenhake, Sweden

Oracle 1989/93 *
Lead, fibreglass
300 x 300 x 300 (p 76)
Courtesy Galerie Nordenhake, Sweden

Augur 1989/93 *
Lead, fibreglass, air, alabaster
300 x 300 x 300, 2 kidneys 35 x 115 x 60 (p 76)
Courtesy Galerie Nordenhake, Sweden

Bridge 1993 *
Lead, fibreglass
330 x 305 x 305 (p 77)
Courtesy Galerie Nordenhake, Sweden

Centre 1993 *
Lead, fibreglass, air, resin
330 x 305 x 305, heart 75 x 100 x 130 (p 77)
Courtesy Galerie Nordenhake, Sweden

Room for the Great Australian Desert 1989
Concrete
920 x 580 x 510 (p 26)
Art Gallery of New South Wales, Sydney

Field for the Art Gallery of New South Wales 1989
Terracotta
230 x 1140 x 10500 (p 28)
Art Gallery of New South Wales, Sydney

Sovereign State 1989/90 *
Brass, lead, plaster, fibreglass, air, rubber hose
Figure: 660 x 1720 x 980; hose: 300 metres long, 35mm diam
(p 48, 92–3)
(Irish Museum of Modern Art)

Seeds V 1989/93 *
Lead
Overall size variable, unit size 35 x 11 diam (frontispiece)
(Malmö Konsthall and Tate Gallery Liverpool)

A Case for an Angel II 1990 *
Plaster, fibreglass, lead, steel, air
1970 x 8580 x 460 (pp 63, 98)
(Malmö Konsthall)
Courtesy Galerie Nordenhake, Sweden

A Case for an Angel III 1990 *
Plaster, fibreglass, lead, steel, air
1970 x 5260 x 350 (pp 46, 99)
(Irish Museum of Modern Art)
Courtesy Salvatore Ala Gallery, New York

Cord 1991
Copper, plaster
3400 x 4 (p 36)

Learning to Think 1991
Lead, fibreglass, air
Five bodycases, each 1730 x 1060 x 310 (pp 37, 67)

Three Bodies 1991
Steel, air
Three spheres, each 1230 diam (p 38)

Host 1991
Mud, sea water
Max depth 130 (p 39)

Fruit 1991
Plaster, oyster shell, mica, wood
Two pieces, each approx 3700 x 2500 x 1550 (p 40)

Still Falling 1991
Cast iron, air
3170 x 2760 x 1480 (p 6)
Collection of Irish Museum of Modern Art, Dublin
(Irish Museum of Modern Art)

Still Running 1990/3 *
Cast iron, air
3170 x 2760 x 1480 (pp 69, 90)
(Malmö Konsthall and Irish Museum of Modern Art)

End Product 1990/3 *
Cast iron, air
2600 x 1100 x 900 (p 87)
(Malmö Konsthall and Irish Museum of Modern Art)

Body 1991/3 *
Cast iron, air
3120 x 2000 x 2900 (pp 30, 88)
(Malmö Konsthall and Irish Museum of Modern Art)

Earth 1991/3 *
Cast iron, air
2600 x 2300 x 2900 (p 89)
(Malmö Konsthall)

Fruit 1991/3 *
Cast iron, air
1040 x 1250 x 1200 (p 86)
(Malmö Konsthall)

Learning to See III 1991
Lead, fibreglass, plaster, air
2180 x 690 x 510 (p 23)
Private Collection, courtesy Galerie Thaddaeus Ropac, Paris

Field 1991
Terracotta (approx 35,000 figures)
Overall size variable, each figure 80–260 (pp 32, 53, 70)
Courtesy Salvatore Ala Gallery, New York

Flesh 1990 *
Concrete
360 x 1980 x 1740 (p 80)
Courtesy Salvatore Ala Gallery, New York

Immersion 1991 *
Concrete
1810 x 505 x 365 (p 78)
Courtesy Salvatore Ala Gallery, New York

Sense 1991 *
Concrete
745 x 625 x 600 (pp 66, 79)
Courtesy Salvatore Ala Gallery, New York

Seeing and Showing 1991/2 *
Lead, fibreglass, plaster
950 x 890 x 450 (p 94)
(Tate Gallery Liverpool)
Private Collection, Cambridge

Home of the Heart I 1992
Concrete
850 x 360 x 550 (p 81)

Home of the Heart II 1992
Concrete
850 x 360 x 550 (p 82)

Home of the Heart III 1992 *
Concrete
850 x 360 x 550 (p 83)

Close I 1992 *
Lead, fibreglass, plaster, air
250 x 1920 x 1860 (pp 62, 91)
(Malmö Konsthall and Tate Gallery Liverpool)
Courtesy Galerie Thaddaeus Ropac, Paris

Close III 1993 *
Cast iron
270 x 2010 x 1740 (p 42)
The Hakone Open-Air Museum, Japan
(Irish Museum of Modern Art)

Testing a World View 1993 *
Cast iron
Five pieces, each 1120 x 470 x 1180 (p 104–7)

European Field 1993 *
Terracotta (approx 40,000 figures)
Overall size variable, each figure 80–260 high (p 100–3)
(Malmö Konsthall)

Field for the British Isles 1993 *
Terracotta (approx 40,000 figures)
Overall size variable, each figure 80–260
(Tate Gallery Liverpool and Irish Museum of Modern Art)
This work is not illustrated.

Antony Gormley

Born in 1950. Lives and works in London.

Solo Exhibitions

1981
Whitechapel Art Gallery, London
Serpentine Gallery, London

1983
Coracle Press, London

1984
Riverside Studios, Hammersmith; Chapter Arts Centre, Cardiff
Salvatore Ala Gallery, New York

1985
Drawings 1981–1985, Salvatore Ala Gallery, New York
Städtische Galerie Regensburg, Regensburg; Frankfurter
Kunstverein, Frankfurt
Galerie Wittenbrink, Munich
Galleria Salvatore Ala, Milan

1986
Salvatore Ala Gallery, New York
Drawings, Victoria Miro Gallery, London

1987
Man Made Man, La Criée, Halle d'art contemporain, Rennes
Drawings, Siebu Contemporary Art Gallery, Tokyo
Vehicle, Salvatore Ala Gallery, New York
Galerie Hufkens de Lathuy, Brussels
Five Works, Serpentine Gallery, London

1988
Burnett Miller Gallery, Los Angeles
Contemporary Sculpture Center, Tokyo
The Holbeck Sculpture, Leeds City Art Gallery, Leeds

1989
Louisiana Museum of Modern Art, Humlebaek
Salvatore Ala Gallery, New York
Scottish National Gallery of Modern Art, Edinburgh
Drawings, McQuarrie Gallery, Sydney
*A Field for the Art Gallery of New South Wales, A Room for the
Great Australian Desert*, Art Gallery of New South Wales, Sydney

1990
Bearing Light, Burnett Miller Gallery, Los Angeles

1991
Drawings and Etchings, Frith Street Gallery, London
Galerie Isy et Christine Brachot, Brussels
Field, Salvatore Ala Gallery, New York
Bearing Light, Shirakawa Gallery, Kyoto
Sculpture, Galerie Nordenhake, Stockholm
Sculptur, Miller Nordenhake, Köln
Field and Other Figures, Modern Art Museum of Fort Worth, Texas

1992
Campo, Centro Cultural Arte Contemporaneo, Mexico City
Field, San Diego Museum of Contemporary Art, La Jolla
Recent Iron Works, Burnett Miller Gallery, Los Angeles
Learning to See, Body & Soul, Contemporary Sculpture Center,
Tokyo
Learning to Think, The British School, Rome

1993
Field, Corcoran Gallery of Art, Washington
Galerie Thaddaeus Ropac, Paris
Field, The Montreal Museum of Fine Arts, Montreal
Galerie Thaddaeus Ropac, Salzburg

Group Exhibitions

* denotes accompanying catalogue

1980
*Nuove Immagine**, Babriele Mazzotta, Milan

1981
*British Sculpture in the Twentieth Century**, Whitechapel Art Gallery, London
*Objects and Sculpture**, Institute of Contemporary Arts, London; Arnolfini Gallery, Bristol

1982
*Figures and Objects: Recent Developments in British Sculpture**, John Hansard Gallery, Southampton
*Objects and Figures**, Fruitmarket Gallery, Edinburgh
Contemporary Choices: CAS Recent Purchases, Serpentine Gallery, London
Whitechapel Open, Whitechapel Art Gallery, London
*Hayward Annual 1982: British Drawing**, Hayward Gallery, London
*Aperto '82**, Biennale di Venezia, Venice

1983
*New Art**, Tate Gallery, London
*The Sculpture Show**, Hayward Gallery and Serpentine Gallery, London
*Whitechapel Open**, Whitechapel Art Gallery, London
*Tongue and Groove**, The Coracle, London
*Assemble Here: Some New British Sculpture**, Puck Building, New York
*Portland Clifftop Sculpture**, Camden Arts Centre, London

1983–4
*Transformations: New Sculpture from Britain**, XVII Bienal de São Paulo; Museu de Arte Moderna, Rio de Janeiro; Museo de Arte Moderno, Mexico City; Museu Calouste Gulbenkian, Lisbon

1984
*1984: An Exhibition**, Camden Arts Centre, London
*An International Survey of Recent Painting and Sculpture**, Museum of Modern Art, New York
*Anni Ottanta**, organised by the Galleria Communale d'Arte Moderna, Bologna; Imola; Ravenna; Rimini
*The British Art Show: Old Allegiances and New Directions 1979–1984**, Birmingham, Sheffield, Edinburgh, Southampton
*Metaphor and/or Symbol: A Perspective on Contemporary Art**, The National Museum of Modern Art, Tokyo; The National Museum of Art, Osaka
*Human Interest**, Cornerhouse, Manchester

1985
*Walking and Falling**, Plymouth Arts Centre, Plymouth; Kettle's Yard, Cambridge; Interim Art, London
*Nuove Trame dell'Arte**, Castello Colonna di Genazzano, Milan
*The British Show**, Art Gallery of New South Wales, Sydney; Art Gallery of Western Australia, Perth; Queensland Art Gallery, Brisbane; National Art Gallery and Wellington Gallery, Wellington

1986
Art and Alchemy, Biennale di Venezia, Venice
*Prospect '86**, Frankfurter Kunstverein, Frankfurt
*The Generic Figure**, Corcoran Gallery of Art, Washington
*Between Object and Image**, Palacio de Velásquez, Parque del Retiro, Madrid; Barcelona; Bilbao
*Vom Zeichnen; Aspekte der Zeichnung 1960–1985**, Franfurter Kunstverein, Frankfurt; Kasseler Kunstverein, Kassel; Museum Moderner Kunst, Vienna

1987
Mitographie: Luoghi Visibili/Invisibile dell'Arte, Pinacoteca Comunale, Ravenna
*Documenta 8**, Kassel
*Avant-Garde in the Eighties**, Los Angeles County Museum of Art, Los Angeles
*T.S.W.A. 3D**, Derry
*The Reemergent Figure**, Storm King Art Center, Mountainville, New York
*State of the Art: Ideas & Images in the 1980s**, Institute of Contemporary Arts, London
*Chaos and Order in the Soul**, University Psychiatric Clinic, Mainz
*Revelation for the Hands**, Leeds City Art Gallery, Leeds; University of Warwick Art Centre, Warwick

1987–8
*Viewpoint**, Musées Royaux des Beaux-Arts de Belgique, Brussels

1988
*The Impossible Self**, Winnipeg Art Gallery, Winnipeg; Vancouver Art Gallery, Vancouver
*Lead**, Hirschl & Adler Modern, New York
*Made to Measure**, Kettle's Yard, Cambridge
*Starlit Waters: British Sculpture, An International Art 1968–1988**, Tate Gallery Liverpool, Liverpool
*ROSC '88** The Guinness Hop Store and the Royal Hospital Kilmainham, Dublin
Porkkana-Kokoelma, Vanhan Galleria, Helsinki, Finland

1988–9
*British Now: sculpture et autres dessins**, Musée d'art contemporain de Montréal, Montreal

1989
It's a Still Life*, Arts Council Collection, The South Bank Centre, London
Objects of Thought, Tornberg Gallery, Lund
Corps-figures*, Art Curial, Paris
Visualization on Paper: Drawing as a Primary Medium, Germans Van Eck, New York

1990
Great Britain – USSR*, Cultural Centre, Kiev; National Cultural Centre, Moscow
Before Sculpture-Sculptors' Drawings, New York Studio School, New York
British Art Now: A Subjective View*, British Council exhibition tour to Japan
Made of Stone*, Galerie Isy Brachot, Brussels

1991
Places with a Past: New Site-Specific Art at Charleston's Spoleto Festival/Sculpture for the Old Jail*, Spoleto Festival USA, Charleston
Inheritance and Transformation*, Irish Museum of Modern Art, Dublin
Goldsmiths' College Centenary Exhibitions 1991*, Goldsmiths' Hall, London
Colours of the Earth, British Council exhibition tour to India and Malaysia

1992
C'est pas la fin du monde*, Rennes; Metz; Caen; Angoulême
Sculpture in the Close*, Jesus College, Cambridge
From the figure, Blum Helman Gallery, New York
Natural Order*, Tate Gallery Liverpool, Liverpool
Des dessins pour les élèves du centre des Deux Thielles, Le Landeron, Centre scolaire et sportif des Deux Thielles, Le Landeron; Öffentliche Kunstsammlung, Museum Für Gegenwartskunst, Basel
Arte Amazonas*, Museu de Arte Moderna, Rio de Janeiro

1993
Vancouver Collects*, The Vancouver Art Gallery, Vancouver
Klima Global: Arte Amazonas*, Staatliche Kunsthalle, Berlin
The Human Factor: Figurative Sculpture Reconsidered*, Albuquerque Museum, Albuquerque
Suite Substitute*, Hotel du Rhone, Geneva
HA HA: Contemporary British Art in an 18th Century Garden, Killerton Park, Devon
Europe sans Frontières, Galerie Isy Brachot, Brussels
Artificial Paradises, Burnett Miller Gallery, Los Angeles
The Fujisankei Biennale, Hakone Open-Air Museum, Japan

Solo Exhibition Catalogues

1981
Antony Gormley, Bulletin Sheet, Whitechapel Art Gallery, London. Text by Jenni Lomax.

1984
Antony Gormley: Drawings From the Mind's Eye, Riverside Studios, Hammersmith; Chapter Arts Centre, Cardiff.

Antony Gormley, Salvatore Ala Gallery, Milan/New York, English and Italian editions. Text by Lynne Cooke.

1985
Antony Gormley: Drawings 1981–1985, Salvatore Ala Gallery, Milan/New York.

Antony Gormley, Städtische Galerie Regensburg, Frankfurter Kunstverein. Text by Veit Loers and Sandy Nairne.

1987
Gormley, The Seibu Department Stores, Tokyo. Text by Michael Newman.
Antony Gormley: Five Works, Serpentine Gallery, London.

1988
Antony Gormley, Contemporary Sculpture Center, Tokyo. Text by Tadayasu Sakai.

1989
Antony Gormley: Sculpture, Louisiana Museum of Modern Art, Humlebaek. Text by Richard Calvocoressi and Oystein Hjort.

'A Field for the Art Gallery of New South Wales / A Room for the Great Australian Desert', Art Gallery of New South Wales, Sydney. Texts by Antony Gormley and Anthony Bond.

1991
Antony Gormley: Field and other figures, Modern Art Museum of Fort Worth, Fort Worth. Artists statements, and texts by Thomas McEvilly and Richard Calvocoressi.

1992
Antony Gormley: Learning to see: Body and Soul, Contemporary Sculpture Center, Tokyo. Text by Masahiro Ushiroshoji.

1993
Learning to see, Galerie Thaddaeus Ropac, Paris/Salzburg. Text by Yehuda Safran, and interview with the artist by Roger Bevan.

Field, The Montreal Museum of Fine Arts, Montreal. Texts by Pierre Théberge, Antony Gormley, Gabriel Orozco and Thomas McEvilley.

Articles and Reviews

1980
'Nuove Immagine', *Flash Art*, Milan, Summer Issue, 1980

1981
Lynne Cooke, 'Antony Gormley at the Whitechapel', *Artscribe*, London, no 29, 1981

Lewis Biggs, 'Objects and Sculpture', *Arnolfini Review*, Bristol, July, 1981

Stuart Morgan, 'Antony Gormley, Whitechapel Gallery', *Artforum*, New York, Summer, 1981

1983
Eli Pascal, 'Tongue and Groove', *Aspects*, Newcastle, Summer, 1983

Michael Newman, 'Man's Place: Four Works', *Art and Artists*, London, 1983

Ramon Tio Bellido, 'Antony Gormley', *Axe-Sud*, Toulouse, Winter, 1983

1984
Nena Dimitrijevic, 'Antony Gormley', *Flash Art*, Milan, January, 1984

Paul Kopecek, 'Antony Gormley Talking to Paul Kopecek', *Aspects*, Newcastle, January, 1984

Nicholas Serota, 'Transformations – New Sculpture from Britain', *Arte Factum*, Antwerp, February/March, 1984

Kim Levin, 'The Clone Zone', *The Village Voice*, New York, May 15, 1984

Beth Biegler, 'Antony Gormley at Salvatore Ala', *The East Village Eye*, New York, June, 1984

William Feaver, 'Variations on a body', *The Observer*, London, September 1984

Margaret Moorman, 'Antony Gormley, Salvatore Ala', *ARTnews*, New York, September, 1984

Gregory Hilty, 'Antony Gormley', *Riverside Studio Bulletin*, London, September, 1984

Marina Vaisey, 'Art & Counterpart', *The Sunday Times*, London, September 16, 1984

William Packer, 'Body building exercises the sculptor's mind', *Financial Times*, London, September 25, 1984

Sanda Miller, 'Antony Gormley at Riverside', *Artscribe*, London, no 49, 1984

Waldemar Januszczak, 'Going up like a lead Balloon', *The Guardian*, London, October 2, 1984

Paul Kopecek, 'Antony Gormley', *Art Monthly*, London, October, 1984

Kate Linker, 'Antony Gormley', *Artforum*, New York, October, 1984

Frederick Ted Castle, 'Antony Gormley at Salvatore Ala', *Art in America*, New York, October, 1984

Charlotte Ducann, 'Interview with Antony Gormley', *World of Interiors*, London, November, 1984

Michael Archer, 'Antony Gormley', *Flash Art*, Milan, December, 1984

1985
Dorothee Müller, 'Schwebende giftige Männer: Antony Gormley in der Müncher Galerie Wittenbrink', *Süddeutsche Zeitung*, Munich, June, 1985

L G Bastos, 'Antony Gormley, a case', *Neue Kunst in Europa*, Munich, no 9, July/August/September, 1985

Rita Pokorny, 'Using the Body as if it was a Face', *Neue Kunst in Europa*, Munich, July/August/September, 1985

Enrico R Comi, 'La quotidianità cosmica del lavoro di Gormley', *Spazio Umano*, Milan, no 3, July/September, 1985

Judith Higgins, 'Antony Gormley', *ARTnews*, New York, December, 1985

Hanne Weskott, 'Antony Gormley', *Kunstforum*, Wetzlar, 1985

1986
Jean Fischer, 'Antony Gormley', *ARTforum*, New York, January, 1986

Gillo Dorfles, 'Antony Gormley', *Italian Vogue*, Milan, February/March, 1986

Paul Richard, 'Upbeat Creature Feature at the Corcoran', *The Washington Post*, March 15, 1986

Kim Levin, 'Chernobyl, Mon Amour', *The Village Voice*, New York, June 24, 1986

Octavio Zaya, 'Antony Gormley: El otro de uno mismo', *Diaro 16*, Madrid, October 26, 1986

Wade Saunders and Anne Rochette, 'Antony Gormley at Salvatore Ala', *Art in America*, New York, November, 1986

1987
'Andrew Graham-Dixon on Antony Gormley's Bizarre Sculptural Techniques', *Harpers & Queen*, London, February, 1987

Waldemar Januszczak, 'British Spirit of Resistance', *The Guardian*, London, March 6, 1987

Sarah Kent, 'In the Lead', *Time Out*, London, March 11, 1987

Richard Cork, 'Figures of Everyman', *The Listener*, London, March 19, 1987

Simon Morley, 'Serpentine Gallery: Antony Gormley', *Artline*, London, April, 1987

Michael Brenson, 'Images that Express Essential Human Emotions', *The New York Times*, July 26, 1987

Mel Gooding, 'Seeing the Sites', *Art Monthly*, London, July/August, 1987

Mina Roustayi, 'An Interview with Antony Gormley', *Arts Magazine*, New York, September, 1987

Mel Gooding, 'Great Britain: TSWA 3D', *Flash Art*, Milan, October 1987

Eric Gibson, 'What's Wrong with The Figure?', *Sculpture*, Washington, November/December, 1987

Judith Higgins, 'Britain's new generation', *Art News*, New York, December, 1987

'Man of Iron', *Stroll*, New York, no 4/5, 1987

1988
Jean-Philippe Lemee, 'Antony Gormley Man Made Man', *Art Press*, Paris, no 119, 1988

Sarah Jane Checkland, 'And the Word was made Art', *The Times*, London, April 2, 1988

James Hamilton, 'The Man's a Brick', *Yorkshire Evening Post*, Leeds, August 19, 1988

'Making the Impossible Self', *Border Crossings*, Winnipeg, Summer, 1988

'Antony Gormley: Kunst in der stadt', *Kassel Kulturell*, September 1988

'Dropping a Brick', *Yorkshire Evening Post*, October 1988

Martin Wainright, 'Northern Brickmanship', *The Guardian*, London, October 17, 1988

Waldemar Januszczak, 'The Might Have Been Man', *The Guardian Weekend*, London, December 17, 1988

1989
Simon Morley, 'Antony Gormley', Tema Celeste, *Siracusa*, Sicily, April/June, 1989

Michael Brenson, 'A sculptor who really gets into his work', *The New York Times*, May 7, 1989

Andrew Graham-Dixon, 'Life set upon a cast', *The Independent*, London, May 9, 1989

Jason Edward Kaufman, 'Antony Gormley's human cyphers', *The New York Tribune*, May 10, 1989

Geraldine Prince, 'A Cast of One', *The List*, Edinburgh, May 18, 1989

Clare Henry, 'Figured out: a way of lifting base metal to artistic heights', *Glasgow Herald*, May 26, 1989

'Antony Gormley', *Art and Design*, London, vol 5, no 3/4, 1989

Clive Turnbull, 'Antony Gormley: The Impossible Self', *The Green Book*, Bristol, vol III, no 1, 1989

Jennifer W Reeves, 'Cast in the sculptor's own mould', *The Christian Science Monitor*, New York, 14 August, 1989

Gretchen Faust, 'New York in review', *Arts Magazine*, New York, September, 1989

Elwyn Lynn, 'The Ambiguity of Intimacy', *The Weekend Australian*, Sydney, November 18–19, 1989

Simon Robinson, 'Making Me Another', *ISIS*, Oxford University, Michaelmas, 1989

1990
Sacha Craddock, 'Derry derring-do', *The Guardian*, London, March 21, 1990

David Pagel, 'Antony Gormley', *Arts Magazine*, New York, April, 1990

Victoria Lynn, 'Earth Above Ground: "Fleshing Out" Antony Gormley', *Art & Text*, Paddington, NSW, Summer, 1990

1991
Michael Brenson, 'Antony Gormley: Salvatore Ala Gallery', *The New York Times Weekend*, March 29, 1991

Michael Brenson, 'Visual Arts join Spoleto Festival U.S.A.', *The New York Times*, May 27, 1991

Barry Schwabsky, 'Antony Gormley', *Arts Magazine*, New York, Summer, 1991

Arthur C Danto, 'Spoleto Festival U.S.A.', *The Nation*, New York, July 29/August 5, 1991

Jane Hart, 'Interview with Antony Gormley', *Journal of Contemporary Art*, New York, vol 4, no 3, Autumn, 1991

Gertrud Sandqvist, 'Människan som blykista', *Svenska Dagbladet*, Stockholm, September 14, 1991

Lars O Erricsson, 'Klafsigt målade träramar och blykroppar', *Dagens Nyheter*, Stockholm, September 17, 1991

Janet Kutner, 'Figuratively speaking', *The Dallas Morning News*, September 28, 1991

Thomas Padon, 'Antony Gormley: Salvatore Ala, New York', *Sculpture*, Washington, September–October, 1991

Bradford R Collins, 'History Lessons' and Robert Taplin, 'Antony Gormley at Salvatore Ala', *Art in America*, New York, November, 1991

Carl-Frederick Harleman and Erik van der Heeg, 'Concentrated spaces', *Material Konst-fanzine*, Stockholm, no 2, 1991

1992
Raquél Tiból, 'Edgar Negret y Antony Gormley en México', *Proceso*, Mexico City, March 9, 1992

Gunter Metken, 'Trauer und Risse im Atelier der Tropen', *Frankfurter Algemeiner Zeitung*, Frankfurt, March 10, 1992

Robert L Pincus, 'Sculptor with earthy world view', *San Diego Union-Tribune*, October 8, 1992

David Pagel, 'Gormley's sculptures get physical', *Los Angeles Times*, October 8, 1992

Kenneth Baker, 'Big theme, tiny figures in San Diego', *San Francisco Chronicle*, October 26, 1992

Enrico Gallian, 'I contenitori dell'ignoto', *L'Unita*, Rome, December 26, 1992

1993
Alisa Tager, 'Reviews: Los Angeles: Antony Gormley', *ARTnews*, New York, January, 1993

Hans Pietch, 'Er ninimt Maß am eigenen Körper', *ART*, Hamburg, March, 1993

Alison Roberts, 'Brummies struggle with metal fatigue', *The Times*, London, April 20, 1993

Hans Janstad, 'Brauda gubbar blir konst', *Arbetet*, Malmö, April 28, 1993

Bernard Paquet, 'Rencontre avec 40,000 figurines: l'art d'Antony Gormley', *Vid Des Arts*, Montreal, May, 1993

Ann Duncan, 'Antony Gormley and the little people', *The Gazette*, Montreal, May 15, 1993

Public Collections

Tate Gallery, London
Victoria and Albert Museum, London
Scottish National Gallery of Modern Art, Edinburgh
Leeds City Art Gallery
Southampton City Art Gallery
Arts Council of Great Britain
British Council
Contemporary Arts Society

Irish Museum of Modern Art, Dublin
Louisiana Museum, Denmark
Marquiles Foundation, Florida
Fort Worth Art Museum
Hakone Open-Air Museum, Ninotaira
Sapporo Sculpture Park, Hokkaido
Neue Galerie, Kassel
Museum of Contemporary Art, Los Angeles
Malmö Konsthall
Walker Arts Centre, Minneapolis
Ville de Rennes
Museum of Contempoary Art, San Diego
Moderna Museet, Stockholm
Art Gallery of New South Wales, Sydney

Photographic Credits

Douglas M Parker Studio, Los Angeles, p65 left
David Ward, pp 25, 46, 53, 63, 74, 75, 76, 77, 78, 79, 80, 81, 82, 83
Edward Woodman p 16
© Isabelle Blondiau p 8
Jan Uvelius, pp 84, 85, 86, 87, 88, 89, 90, 91, 100, 101, 102, 103, 104,
105, 106, 107
John McWilliams, pp 36, 37, 38, 39, 40
Joseph Coscia jr, p 32
Louis Bustamante p 59
Tate Gallery Photographic Department, pp 14, 51, 65 right, 67 right
Thomas Photography, p 60
Witt Library, p 64 right
All other photographs by the artist

Reproduction Permissions

Jacob Epstein *Elemental* is reproduced by permission of a private
collection
Jacob Epstein *Lazarus* is reproduced by permission of the Warden
and Fellows, New College, Oxford
Robert Morris *The Ells* is reproduced by courtesy of Margo Leavin
Gallery, Los Angeles
Sebastiano del Piombo *The Raising of Lazarus* is reproduced by
courtesy of the Trustees, The National Gallery of London
Tony Smith *Die* is reproduced by courtesy of Paula Cooper
Gallery, New York

This book is published to accompany three exhibitions of the work of Antony Gormley
organised by Malmö Konsthall, Tate Gallery Liverpool and the
Irish Museum of Modern Art.

Malmö Konsthall 18 September – 31 October 1993
Tate Gallery Liverpool 20 November 1993 – 6 February 1994
Irish Museum of Modern Art 14 April – 19 June 1994

ISBN 91 7704 061 9   Malmö Konsthall (Swedish)
ISBN 1 85437 128 2   Tate Gallery (English)

Prepared by Tate Gallery Liverpool and published by
Tate Gallery Publications, Millbank, London SW1P 4RG

Edited by Judith Nesbitt
Prepared by Jemima Pyne and Helen Ruscoe
Designed by Herman Lelie
Typeset by Goodfellow and Egan, Cambridge
Printed in Great Britain by Balding + Mansell, Wisbech